REFASHIONED BAGS

UPCYCLE ANYTHING INTO HIGH-STYLE HANDBAGS

FAITH & JUSTINA BLAKENEY

POTTER
CRAFT

new york

To Mom, Dad, Grandma Bette, and Grandpa Art for always nurturing and supporting all of our outlandish creative endeavors.

Copyright © 2009 by Faith Blakeney and Justina Blakeney

All rights reserved.

Published in the United States by Potter Craft, an imprint of the Crown Publishing Group, a division of Random House, Inc., New York.
www.crownpublishing.com
www.pottercraft.com

POTTER CRAFT and colophon is a registered trademark of Random House, Inc.

Library of Congress Cataloging-in-Publication Data

Blakeney, Faith.
   Refashioned bags : upcycle anything into high-style handbags /
Faith Blakeney and Justina Blakeney. — 1st ed.
      p.   cm.
   Includes index.
   ISBN 978-0-307-46088-2
   1. Handbags. I. Blakeney, Justina. II. Title.
   TT667.B62   2009
   646.4'8—dc22   2009005017

Printed in China

Project photography by Philip Touitou
Photography page 69 by Jodi Bates © Gossip Gossip
Design and illustrations by Faith and Justina Blakeney
Styling by Jen Ng
Technical editing by Alicia Zenobia

10 9 8 7 6 5 4 3 2 1

First Edition

CONTENTS

4 SMALL BAGS & CLUTCHES

INTRODUCTION

After showing you *99 Ways* to cut up your T-shirt, deck out your denim, and rock your scarf, we, the Compai sisters, are at it again. *Refashioned Bags* is a book that provides you with the know-how to make stylish bags out of items you can readily find in your home. Recycling and reappropriating everyday items into designer accessories is fun, cheap, easy, and oh-so-eco!

But have no fear; you need not be a seamstress or a metalsmith to make it happen. This book, like recycling, is for everybody. Our twenty-four simple how-to projects contain detailed instructions, helpful facts, and fun illustrations for crafters of all skill levels. A glossary explains sewing terms and techniques, and a resource page provides lots of handy contacts for materials and inspiration. With just a few basic tools and a spare afternoon, you'll be making everyday bags, utility bags, totes and shoppers, clutches, and other small bags for special occasions.

We have also handpicked the hottest and most innovative bags made from post-consumer materials from around the globe. The designers of these bags contribute their stories, tips on sourcing, and their artistic pitfalls and triumphs for your crafty inspiration.

So it's time to get creative, clean out the closets, and discover what hidden treasures lie within. Your wardrobe, your wallet, and your planet will thank you.

Love, Faith & Justina

TOOL KEY

HOT GLUE GUN

TAILOR'S CHALK

SEWING MACHINE

SCISSORS

CRAFT KNIFE

MASKING TAPE

IRON

NEEDLE & THREAD

STAPLER

HOW TO USE THIS BOOK

We all have clutter and cast-offs, and we all use bags. So why not turn that "junk" into a useful handbag or two (or three or . . .)? This book provides you with all the instructions, techniques, incentive, and inspiration you'll need. It is a roadmap for adventurous upcyclers on their journey to a fabulous, new, refashioned world. As with all journeys, this one begins with a first step.

Start here:

1. Use this book without caution. You have nothing to lose but your "junk."

2. Scavenge your closets, drawers, and garage (and your friends', too, if they are game)!

3. This is the hard part: Choose a bag to start with from *Refashioned Bags*—twenty-four rockin' DIY projects.

4. Novice? Note the stars on each project; they indicate level of difficulty from 1 (easy) to 4 (challenging). There are also no-sew projects for non-sewers!

5. Use the simple instructions and illustrations to create your dream bag.

6. Need extra help? All of the glossary terms throughout the book are in boldface type. Consult the Glossary of Techniques (page 108).

7. Wear it. Own it. Flaunt it. Recycle it. Sell it. Pass it on.

8. To see what other pros in the industry are up to, peruse the designer features.

9. Use the suggested techniques to create your own designs. Once you have the skills, why not make a Plastic Bag Fusion Shopper, or a Curtain Messenger Bag?

10. For a little more incentive (as if you need it), check out the nifty facts in the margins, as well as the Recycler's Resources at the back of the book (page 110).

11. Most importantly, have fun, take risks, and be resourceful—and if you want to share your creations and ideas, check out the Compai blog (compai.blogspot.com) and join the Compai Community of revolutionary recyclers!

 STARS INDICATE LEVEL OF DIFFICULTY: * = EASY, **** = CHALLENGING
All bag dimensions are listed as length x height x depth.

CHAPTER 1

EVERYDAY BAGS

During the day, we need comfy bags that balance fashion and function. We would all love to carry clutches to work and fancy, sparkly, blinged-out bags to the library, but let's face it—that's just not practical. So in this chapter we've created daytime bags for schlepping in style. These bags can hold more than just an ID, keys, and a lipstick. They are big enough to tote around laptops and smart enough for a stroll through the Museum of Modern Art. The **Cravat Carryall** is not only adorable, but it's also a perfect post-breakup bag to make from your ex's work ties. The **Tux Redux Bag** is professional and au courant—great for a job interview. We guarantee that whatever you are doing during the day, people will stop and ask you, "Where did you get that gorgeous bag?" In fact, we suggest making business cards that say, "I made it myself." (Check out page 112.)

LE ZIP SAC PG. 24

CRAVAT CARRYALL

YOU'LL NEED

- 8 old neckties

- scrap of woven fabric, 12" x 12" (30.5cm x 30.5cm)

- Piece of cardboard at least 12" x 12" (30.5cm x 30.5cm)

- Lots of space (try working this project out on the floor)

- Pins

DIMENSIONS

9" x 14" (23cm x 35.5cm)

1. Cut 6 of the ties off at the thin end so each is 26" (66cm) long. Leave 2 ties uncut.

2. To make the bottom of the bag, create a "cross" shape by laying the wide tips of the 2 uncut ties tip to tip, forming a straight horizontal line from left to right. Lay 2 of the 26"- (66cm-) long ties vertically at the center of this horizontal line, with the wide tips meeting those of the horizontal ties. Using a sewing machine, sew the wide tips together with a **clean finish.**

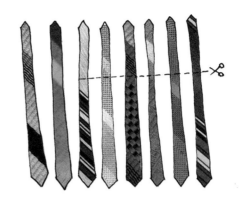

3. Lay each remaining tie between the sewn ties, with the wide tips at the center. **Pin** the tips into place.

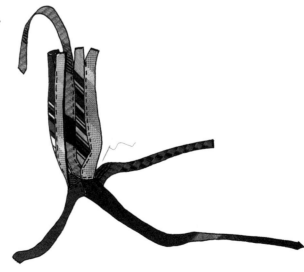

4. With all 8 ties in place, sew the tips and then the sides of the ties together, edge to edge, with a clean finish to create a bucket shape. Leave the top 4" (10cm) of the 26" (66cm) ties unsewn.

TIE ENVY

We love working with ties because their similar shapes and lengths fit together nicely. They're also easy to find in bulk. When scavenging for ties, choose those with similar color palettes to unify their often outrageous patterns. Such bold contrasts are fit for any season.

QUICK TIP: We suggest ironing the seams before and after sewing each necktie. It will ensure that everyone knows the bag was made by you, not your baby sister.

RECYCLE IT: Don't forget to recycle the remnants! Use leftover pieces of the ties to make bracelets. Trim leftovers to the length of the circumference of your wrist, adding about ½" (13mm). Hem the raw edge, sew a button on one end, put a corresponding button-hole at the other, and button it on!

5. **Hem** the top edge of the 26" (66cm) ties. (Do not hem the top of the 2 long ties.)

6. From the cardboard, cut out a circle with a diameter of 10" (25.5cm). Then cut an 11" (28cm) diameter circle from the scrap of fabric. Using the hot glue gun, glue the fabric circle to the cardboard, folding the edges of the fabric over the edges of the cardboard to create a smooth, finished, fabric-covered circle.

7. Using the cardboard circle as a template, place it against the bottom of the bag. Pinch and pin the fabric around the edge of the cardboard circle, creating what will look like circular piping around the bottom of the bag. Remove the cardboard and **topstitch** around the pinned fabric edge to define the circular bottom of the bag.

8. Apply glue to the back of the cardboard circle and glue it to the inside bottom of the bag.

9. Knot the 2 long ties at the top of the bag to create an adjustable strap.

ASHLEY WATSON {designer feature}

A true recycler knows that even Dad's crusty old hand-me-downs can become killer accessories. "It was actually an accident," says designer Ashley Watson of the refashioned bag that launched her career as an independent handbag designer. "I was at my parent's house about four years ago and wanted to make myself a handbag. I found a leather jacket of my dad's, so I cut it up and made a bag out of it. I ended up really liking the result."

And so this "accidental" handbag led to another, and another. Now, with a thriving wholesale handbag business, Watson hunts for leather in charity thrift stores and rag warehouses. "I enjoy using recycled leather because it has a history and makes each bag one-of-a-kind . . . But finding the right jackets is becoming a challenge," she says. "They can't be too expensive, must be in good condition, and be available in popular colors." However challenging, we're pretty sure that most people would prefer hunting for leather in thrift shops to hunting for it on the range. We love Watson because not only does she name her bags after really cute songbirds (like the Warbler bag, shown here), but she also creates ethically responsible design without compromising an ounce of style.

➕ When sewing by machine on leather, use a heavy thread, a leather needle, and as little tension as possible.

♻ When recycling old leather garments, reuse the original detailing as much as possible. For example, use the waistband of leather pants as handles, use existing buttons and buttonholes for new closures, and strategically place existing seams to enhance the design details.

Name
Ashley Watson

URL
ashleywatson.net

Occupation
Handbag Designer

Age
29

Location
Vancouver,
British Columbia,
Canada

Bag Description
One-of-a-kind
"Warbler" recycled
leather bag

Key Techniques
Reusing leather
clothing and
transforming it into
handbags

TUX REDUX BAG

YOU'LL NEED

- 1 old tuxedo jacket (a regular suit jacket can also be used)
- Cotton filling or batting
- Pins
- Seam ripper

DIMENSIONS

13" x 15" (33cm x 38cm)

1. Remove all buttons on the jacket (EXCEPT the ones on the sleeves) and set them aside. Starting 4" (10cm) under the armpit, cut across the jacket to cut off the bottom portion. Cut off the right sleeve at the armpit level and the left sleeve 10" (25.5cm) from the cuff.

2. Lay the bottom piece of jacket flat and cut vertically 1" (2.5cm) from the left side of the right pocket. Set this small rectangle aside.

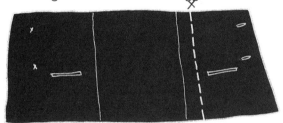

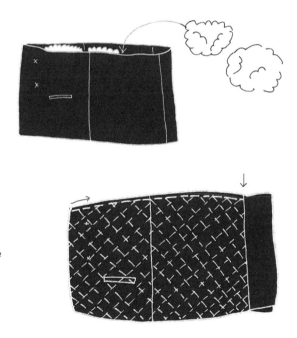

3. Evenly place about 6 handfuls of cotton filling between the lining and the outside fabric of the larger portion of the jacket bottom. **Pin** in place.

4. Fold all open edges under and **topstitch** closed. Then sew crisscrossing diagonal lines to **quilt** the fabric, sewing over the existing pocket.

5. Fold this quilted rectangle in half lengthwise, then rotate so the bag's pocket line is vertical.

6. To make the pocket for the bag, open up the left (shorter) sleeve at the back seam and remove the lining. Aligning the bottom edge of the sleeve with the bottom edge of the bag, pin the sleeve into the bottom left side seam of the bag. **Tuck** and **gather** the bottom, and pin into place. Sew along the right edge and the bottom edge of the pocket to secure.

7. Cut the remaining sleeve into 2 equal-length pieces, each about 13" x 4½" (33cm x 12cm). Turn each piece inside out, sew with a ¾" (2cm) seam allowance to create a tube, and turn back to the right side. Tuck in the ends of the tube and topstitch along all 4 sides to flatten the tubes into straps.

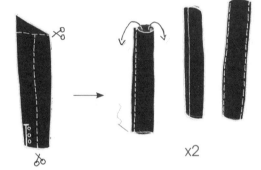

x2

8. To attach the straps, position the buttoned cuff over the front of the bag, about 2" (5cm) from the left edge of the bag. Make sure that at least 3½" (9cm) of the strap overlaps the front edge for strength. Sew into place. At the same depth, position and pin the opposite end of the strap against the inside front of the bag, 2" (5cm) from the right edge so that the strap is centered on the bag. Sew into place. Using these measurements, pin and sew the other strap to the inside back of the bag.

front view

back view

9. Cut out two 7" x 4½" (18cm x 12cm) rectangles from the fabric set aside in step 2, centering each on a buttonhole. Sew the rectangles closed to make 2 tubes, following the instructions from step 7 to turn each tube into a flat strap. If you do not have any buttonholes in your fabric, then **make buttonholes** at the ends of the straps.

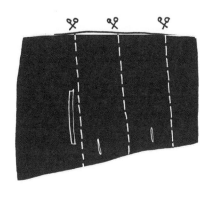

10. Sew the straps to the back of the bag with a clean finish as desired.

back view

11. With the bag folded, right side in, sew both sides closed, being sure to seal the pocket pinned in place in step 6. **Sew 2 buttons** (reserved in step 1) on the front of the bag so that the side straps can be buttoned.

JAZZED-UP JACKET

A tuxedo makes a lasting impression, but what if your tux goes out of style or just doesn't fit like it use to? Take that powder blue '70s special somewhere other than the cleaners. This project will transform your less-than-lux tux into a go-anywhere accessory sure to make a lasting impression yet again—this time without all the ruffles.

QUICK TIP: Often, tuxedos have very fine detailing. If your tux boasts beautiful lapels, adorned buttons, and special stitches or lining, make sure to incorporate them into your bag's design.

RECYCLE IT: Don't have a tuxedo to recycle? With more than 6,200 weddings a day in the United States, finding an abandoned tuxedo in your local thrift store should be a breeze, but you can also adapt this project to any suit jacket.

BATH MAT BAG-IT

YOU'LL NEED

- 2 rubber bath mats of contrasting colors
- 6 shower-curtain rings
- Hole puncher
- Rubber cement glue

DIMENSIONS

10" x 10½" (25.5cm x 26.5cm)

1. Cut a 24" x 10" (61cm x 25.5cm) rectangle (piece **A**) out of 1 bath mat.

2. From the other bath mat, cut out 2 rectangles, each 12" x 4" (30.5cm x 10cm), (**B**) and (**C**). Cut out 1 square piece, 9" x 9" (23cm x 23cm), (**D**); and 2 long, thin strips 13" x 1½" (33cm x 3.8cm), (**E**) and (**F**).

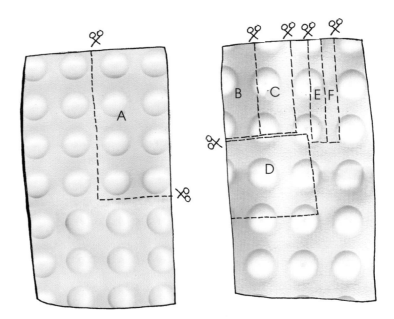

3. Fold piece (**A**) in half lengthwise, right side in. Place piece (**B**) (right side in) onto the left side of piece (**A**), as shown, and staple in place with a few staples.

4. Place piece (**C**) onto the right side of piece (**A**) (right side in), and staple in place with a few staples.

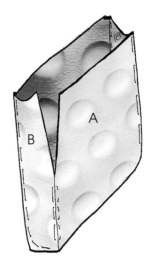

5. Spread an even layer of rubber cement glue on the "seams" between pieces (**A**) and (**B**) and pieces (**A**) and (**C**), covering the staples completely.

6. Wait for the glue to dry, then turn the bag right side out and staple 1 side of square (**D**) to the top, back side of piece (**A**). Reinforce the seam with rubber cement.

RUBBER REMIX

This is not just a water resistant wonder bag. It is also yet another perfect example of upcycling, taking something disposable and turning it into an object of lasting value. Take these bath mats for example, dime a dozen. But with a few staples and swipes of rubber cement, you'll create a bag with true value. See, you are not only a recycler but you are also an upcycler—and you didn't even know it!

QUICK TIP: If you don't have rubber cement, try using duct tape to line the inside of the bag and protect your precious, crafty hands from potentially pokey staples.

RECYCLE IT: Stuck with leftover bath mat pieces? Make yourself a matching change purse! Cut out 1 rectangle and fold it lengthwise (right-side in), making sure 1 side is 1" (2.5cm) longer than the other (for the flap). Staple the sides together, flip right-side out, and sew on a snap.

7. Punch a hole in the top center of piece (**B**) and another in the top center of piece (**C**).

8. Punch a hole on each end of pieces (**E**) and (**F**). Now glue pieces (**E**) and (**F**) on top of each other. Be sure to match up the pieces exactly, including the holes, so that the curtain rings can go through the holes easily.

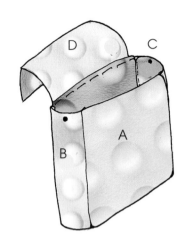

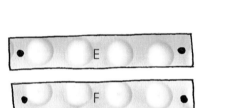

9. Place 3 of the shower-curtain rings 1 inside the other, creating a 3-ringed chain. Repeat with the remaining 3 rings. Fasten the first 3-ringed chain to piece (**B**) through the hole. Next, fasten the second 3-ringed chain to piece (**C**) through the hole.

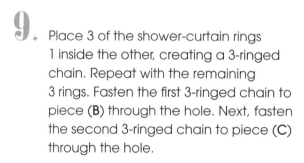

10. Fasten the curtain rings through the holes in (**E**) and (**F**), completing the strap of the bag.

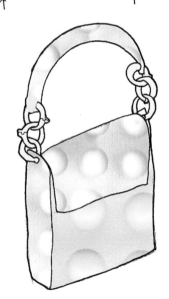

TRIPP WORX {designer feature}

Tripp Gregson is a rebel *with* a cause! Using traffic signs as the primary material for his creations, Gregson recycles while poking fun at authority by cutting up signs. His approach to the material is very hands on; like a sculptor, he twists and turns them every which way, exploring shapes and dimensions until he creates something that speaks to him.

Gregson finds his traffic signs in scrap yards. He asserts that "recycled materials have experience . . . this look . . . one can tell they're real, they've got depth . . . sometimes the colors are a bit faded, sometimes there's a scratch or a dent, or sometimes they have a bullet hole." Gregson has a passion for traffic signs because he says they have the power to make "a bold iconographic statements that juxtaposes colorful graphics in an unexpected way."

Name
Tripp Gregson

Company
Tripp WorX

URL
trippworx.com

Location
Greensboro, North Carolina

Bag Description
Recycled aluminum traffic signs, vinyl remnants from furniture factories, and a clasp crafted from the top of an Austin-Healey sports car make up the bags

Design Philosophy
To make something out of nothing

Key Techniques
Cutting, Riveting

➕ Gregson broke into the industry by selling his work at art galleries. There are no limits to the market when it comes to selling your recycled creations—they are art!

♺ Junkyards are great places to find materials and inspiration for dirt-cheap prices—from cool hardware to old rubber or metal parts.

WOVEN WASHER BAG

YOU'LL NEED

- 46 nickel washers, 1¼" (3cm) in diameter

- Scrap of woven (nonstretch) fabric, at least 24" x 60" (61cm x 152.5cm)

- Wide ribbon (old seatbelts, waist belts, or neck ties of a similar width would also do the trick), at least 94" x 3½" (239cm x 9cm)

- Pins

DIMENSIONS

9½" x 13" (24cm x 33cm)

1. From the scrap fabric, cut eight, 20" x 5" (51cm x 12.5cm) strips and eight, 10" x 5" (25.5cm x 12.5cm) strips.

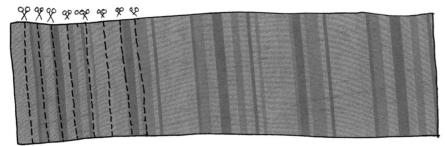

2. Fold 1 strip in half widthwise with right sides in and sew along the long edge to create a tube. Turn the tube inside out so the seams are on the inside. Repeat this process with the 15 remaining fabric strips.

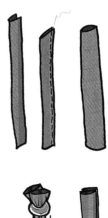

3. Thread 1 long tube through the hole in a washer. Fold the fabric tube in half, and place the washer at the fold. Now thread both ends of the fabric through another washer.

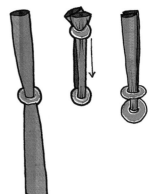

4. Thread 1 of the short fabric tubes through the hole in the bottom washer, fold the shorter fabric tube in half, and thread another washer over both ends of the shorter tube. Now slip the final washer over 1 end of the shorter tube, then tie the short tube in a tight knot at the bottom.

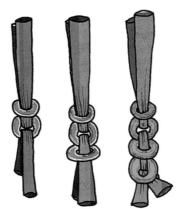

5. Repeat steps 3–4 with the remaining strips.

6. Cut out a 28" x 20" (71cm x 51cm) rectangle from the fabric.

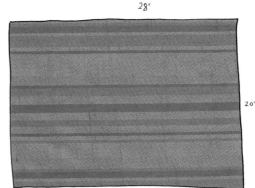

7. Fold the fabric in half lengthwise, right side facing in, and sew along the long edge to create a tube. Turn the fabric right side out and fold the open ends of the top and bottom ½" (13mm) inward so that no raw edges are visible; **pin** into place.

8. Fold the tube in half widthwise and sew up both sides, creating a large pocket, which will become the body of the bag.

9. Place 1 of the folded fabric tubes around the base of the large pocket so that the washers dangle. One end of the fabric tube will be at the back of the bag and the other end will be in front. Pin the base, top front, and top back of the tube to the pocket with 1 pin each. Repeat, spacing tubes evenly, until all 8 fabric tubes are pinned onto the pocket in a row.

10. **Topstitch** all along the bottom of the pocket, fastening the tubes in place in front and back.

11. Thread 1 washer onto every tube that is on the front of the bag.

12. Cut a 19" (48.5cm) length of the 3½"- (9cm-) wide ribbon and weave it through the tubes at the base of the bag, in front and back until the ribbon ends meet at the side of the bag. **Hand-stitch** the ribbon ends together.

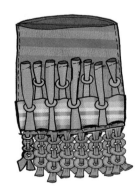

13. Cut another 19" (48.5 cm) length of ribbon and place it directly above the first ribbon. Weave the ribbon through the tubes. Where the first ribbon is woven under, the second ribbon should weave over. Hand-stitch the ribbon closed once the beginning of the ribbon reaches the end, on the back.

14. Fold the tips of all of the tubes down behind the ribbon and pin into place, then hand-stitch all the way across, sewing the ribbon to the tubes and the tubes to the outermost layer of the pocket, all the way around. Make sure you do not sew straight through to the other side of the bag.

15. Cut 40" (101.5cm) of the 3½"- (9cm-) wide ribbon and thread 6 washers onto it. Place 1 end of the ribbon into the left corner of the pocket, in between the outermost layer and the first inside layer, and pin into place. Place the other end of the ribbon into the right corner, in between the opposite outermost layer and the second inside layer, and pin into place.

16. Sew around the entire top edge of the bag, securing the straps into place and hemming the top edge simultaneously.

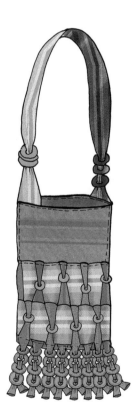

HEAVY METALS

Tough and ready for anything, the Woven Washer Bag is heavy metal without the whiplash. Fabric choice for this bag, like earplugs at a Metallica concert, will determine your long-term success (and ability to hear all those compliments you'll be getting with this bag in tow). We recommend thick, sturdy fabrics patterned with a subtle graphic pattern like stripes to balance the weight and shine of the washers.

QUICK TIP: A hardware store can be an upcycler's best friend. We plucked the washers shown in this project from among the hundreds of shiny nuts, bolts, and thingamabobs in our local hardware store. We chose nickel washers to coordinate with our fabric, but you might prefer brass, bronze, or even copper.

RECYCLE IT: Got a few extra washers? String them together with a nylon thread to make a funky chunky bracelet or necklace!

LE ZIP SAC

YOU'LL NEED

- 10 zippers, at least 12" (30.5cm) long
- 34" (86cm) zipper
- Scrap fabric (we used fabric from an old pillow sham)
- 1 length of sturdy chain at least 10" (25.5cm) long
- A jump ring and clasp
- Thick, nylon thread
- Thimble
- Pins

DIMENSIONS

13" x 8½" (33cm x 21.5cm)

1. Cut two 22" x 12" (56cm x 30.5cm) rectangles from the fabric.

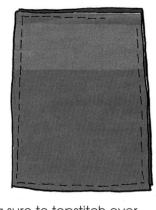

2. Place the 2 rectangles face to face, and sew them together around the perimeter, leaving a 2" (5cm) opening at the top so you can turn the fabric right side out.

3. Turn the fabric right side out, making sure to pull out all 4 corners so that they are pointy (not rounded).

4. **Topstitch** around the perimeter of the rectangle ¼" (6mm) from the edge, making sure to topstitch over the 2" (5cm) opening that was left in step 2.

5. Fold the rectangle in half widthwise and draw a line at the middle of the fabric with chalk.

chalk line

6. Open your first 12" (30.5cm) zipper, and cut off the stop, splitting the zipper into 2. Put the top half along the top edge of the chalk line, zipper teeth facing down. **Pin** in place.

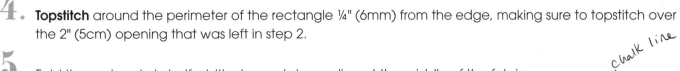

7. Repeat with 7 zippers. Each should be placed 1 just above the other (not overlapping), with the teeth facing down until you reach the 11th zipper half.

8. Using a zipper foot, sew the first zipper half onto the rectangle. Continue up the fabric, sewing on the zipper halves.

9. Now, instead of a zipper half, topstitch a whole zipper onto the fabric. Open the zipper.

10. Cut open the fabric inside the zipper's opening, leaving 1" (2.5cm) of fabric uncut on either end.

11. Cut out one 11" x 8" (28cm x 20.5cm) piece of fabric. Fold it in half lengthwise (right side in) and sew the 2 ends with a **clean finish** about 3" (7.5cm) from the folded edges toward the open edge, creating a pocket.

12. Place the pocket inside of the slit created in step 10, and pin it into place. Sew the long sides of the pocket to the top and bottom edges of the slit with a clean finish. Then sew the sides shut.

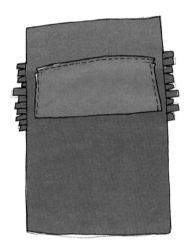

13. Sew 4 more half zippers (teeth down) onto the front of the rectangle, above the pocket.

14. Fold the rectangle in half lengthwise (zipper side in) and match up the 4 corners of the bag. Pin in place.

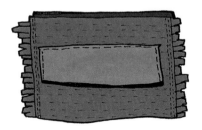

15. Using a small needle and a thimble to sew small stitches, **hand-stitch** up the sides of the bag. Sew over the zippers as you go. Reinforce the seams with another row of small stitches on each side. Turn the bag so that the zippers are facing out.

16. Using a zipper foot, sew the last 12" (30.5cm) zipper into the inside of the opening of the top of the bag.

17. Cut a 34" x 5" (86cm x 12.5cm) piece of fabric. Fold the fabric in half widthwise and sew the 2 sides together with a clean finish, creating a tube. Using a safety pin, turn the tube right side out and iron flat.

18. Topstitch the 34" (86cm) zipper onto the tube. **Hem** the short sides.

19. Hand-stitch the strap to the bottom right corner of the bag. Reinforce with extra stitches. Hand-stitch the strap to the right, top corner of the bag, as shown.

20. Lastly, hand-stitch the other end of the strap to the left corner of the bag, and use the jump ring to attach the chain to the zipper pull that opens the pocket.

OPEN SHUT CASE

This bag is not only a recycled masterpiece (if we do say so ourselves) . . . it is also an homage to one of Compai's favorite fashion revolutionaries, Yohji Yamamoto, a pioneering Japanese designer who designed an ab fab collection in 1998 primarily using zippers. We love it!

QUICK TIP: We used leftover zippers from our clothing collections to make this bag, but you could recycle old zippers by cutting them off of sweatshirts and jackets! Just unzip the garment and cut each half to 12" (30.5cm).

FUN FACT: Though the earliest patent for a "continuous clothing closure" appeared in 1851, the zipper as we know it today didn't appear on the scene until some sixty years later, when an updated version appeared on rubber boots and tobacco pouches, protecting their contents against the elements.

CHAPTER 2

UTILITY BAGS

Why sacrifice aesthetics for practicality when you can have it all? Utility bags are notoriously unsightly, but we all need a few. They protect our computers, carry our baby gear, and tote our school books. This chapter shows you how to make the bags that you need, and it won't take you long to realize they are the bags you want, too! The **Sweater Computer Cozy** turns a shrunken sweater into a sweet laptop cover (heck, your little sister wouldn't wear that thing; why not hand-me-down-it to your beloved computer?), while the **Dapper Diaper Bag** transforms Grandma's old, torn-up quilt into Mommy's favorite baby carryall! These bags, born of a necessity for comfort, durability, and practicality, are accessories that will get you excited about toting around all your stuff! See? You can have it all.

SWEATER COMPUTER COZY PG. 38

DENIM BACKPACK

✳ ✳ ✳ ✳

YOU'LL NEED

- 2 old articles of denim clothing with contrasting colors or patterns (We used 2 pairs of jeans so we each had a pair of shorts after the project was completed.)

- Pins

DIMENSIONS

12" x 15" x 3½" (30.5cm x 38cm x 9cm)

1. From the first article of denim, cut out one 12" x 6" (30.5cm x 15cm) rectangle, piece (**A**); two 14" x 5" (35.5cm x 12.5cm) rectangles, (**B**) and (**C**); one 14" x 12" (35.5cm x 30.5cm) rectangle, (**D**); and one 19" x 13" (48.5cm x 33cm) rectangle, (**E**).

2. From the second article, cut off the waistband, (**F**); two 30" x 3" (76cm x 7.5cm) strips, (**G**) and (**H**); and one 9" x 12" (23cm x 30.5cm) rectangle, (**I**).

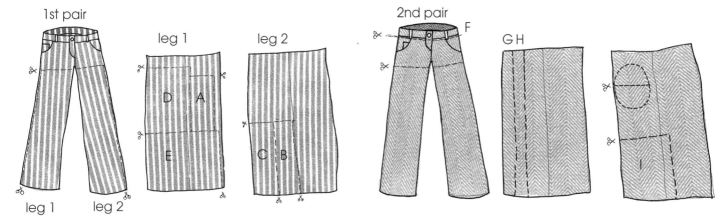

3. Cut an 8" (20.5cm) long piece, including the button-hole, from waistband (**F**). **Hem** the raw edge and set aside. Measuring from the raw edge of the waistband (**F**), cut off a 6" (15cm) long piece to create piece (**J**). **Gather** piece (**I**) underneath piece (**J**), as shown. Sew piece (**J**) onto piece (**I**) and **clean finish** the edges.

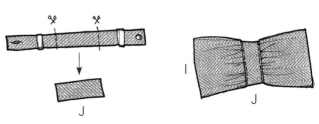

4. Place piece (**I**) at the bottom of piece (**D**), lining up the 12" (30.5cm) ends. **Pin** into place. Hem the top edge of piece (**D**), creating the font piece of the backpack.

5. From the remaining fabric of the second article of denim, cut out 2 half circles, 6½" x 5" (16.5cm x 12.5cm), then create a **curved seam** on the rounded edges of both half circles, as shown.

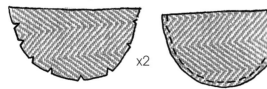

6. Place the half circles onto piece (D) directly above piece (I), as illustrated, creating covers for the outside pocket. Pin into place with the flat edges of the half circles folded under for a clean finish. Sew the half circles onto piece (D).

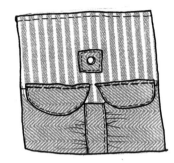

7. Cut out the button from waistband (F) centered on a 2" x 2" (5cm x 5cm) denim square. Hem the raw edge. Place the denim square in the center of piece (D), 1" (2.5cm) directly above the half circles, as shown. Sew the button square into place.

8. Sew the short ends of pieces (B), (A), and (C) together (in that order) with a clean finish, then hem the 2 remaining short edges on pieces (B) and (C).

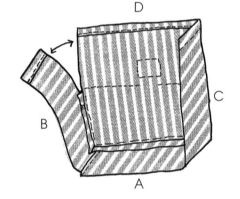

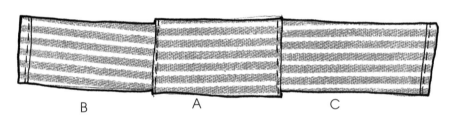

9. Pin piece (B, A, C) to the edge of piece (D), all the way around, so that piece (A) is along the bottom and pieces (B) and (C) are along the sides of piece (D), creating the sides of the bag. Sew (B, A, C) to (D) with a clean finish. Be sure that the side and bottom edges of piece (I) are sewn into the seams, sealing the 1 large pocket.

10. Cut 2 right triangles, 3" x 2" (7.5cm x 5cm), off each top corner of piece (E), as shown. Hem around the top edge triangle notches and the 2 sides of piece (E). Hem both long sides on strips (G) and (H).

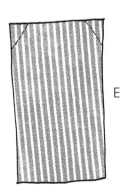

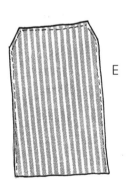

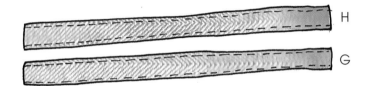

H

G

11. Pin (**G**) and (**H**) to piece (**E**), 2" (5cm) from the bottom and 4" (10cm) apart from each other to create the backpack straps. Be sure to fold the short, raw edges inward. Once in place, sew the straps to the bottom of piece (**E**), sewing several times over the seam to be sure that the straps are secure.

12. Repeat this process with the opposite ends of pieces (**G**) and (**H**), sewing (**G**) and (**H**) onto (**E**), 7½" (19cm) from the top, and 6" (15cm) apart, to secure both straps into place.

13. Cut a 12"- (30.5cm-) long strip from waistband (**F**). Pin both ends of the strip horizontally onto (**E**), 2½" (6.5cm) from the side edges of piece (**E**) and 5" (12.5cm) from the top (directly above straps (**G**) and (**H**)). Sew in a 1"- (2.5cm-) wide square on both ends of the strap to fasten the 12" (30.5cm) strip to piece (**E**). This creates a loop at the top of the bag to hang the bag from or to carry it with.

14. Place the 8"- (20.5cm-) long strip cut from waistband (**F**) in step 3 vertically (with the buttonhole at the top) along the center of piece (**E**), just above the loop that was created in step 13. Let 2" (5cm) (the end with the buttonhole) extend past the edge of piece (**E**).

15. Align the outer edge of piece (**B, A, C**) with the bottom edge of piece (**E**), and then sew the sides and bottom to complete the pack. Now give yourself a pat on the back and go to class!

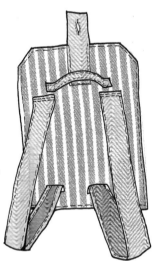

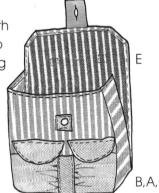

E

B, A, C

JEAN-IE IN A BAG

When you're looking for comfort and utility in a bag, nothing quite beats the good ol' backpack. And when you are looking for the same thing in a fabric, nothing quite does it like denim. So, ladies and gentleman, we proudly present to you the greatest backpack on the planet— it's cute too!

QUICK TIP: We recommend using 2 contrasting colors of denim, or at least different shades, for a funky look. Also, make sure to use a denim needle in your sewing machine—it will be a worthy investment for this project, promise!

RECYCLE IT: Don't toss the leftover denim pieces! Use the scraps to make anything from letter carriers to slippers. Visit our blog at compai.blogspot.com or check out our book *99 Ways to Cut, Sew & Deck Out Your Denim* for oodles of inspiration.

CARGO CARRYALL

YOU'LL NEED

- 1 pair of cargo pants

- 1 yard (91cm) scrap stretch fabric (We used a polyester jersey top from the '70s.)

- Pins

DIMENSIONS

16" x 13" x 4½" (40.5cm x 33cm x 11.5 cm)

1. Cut the cargo pants across the legs just under the fly and just above the knee, in front and back. The length of the pieces with the pockets should be about 14" (35.5cm).

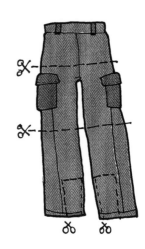
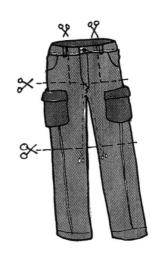

2. Take the pieces with pockets and cut up the inner thigh seams to make 2 rectangular pieces, each with a large cargo pocket. Trim the sides so the rectangles are even in size.

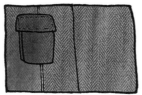

3. Sew the ends of the rectangles together with a **clean finish**, creating a tube.

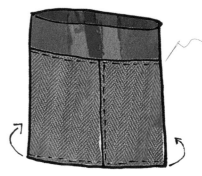

4. Cut a piece from the scrap fabric that is the same circumference as the tube and 5" (12.5cm) wide. **Hem** 1 long edge of the scrap fabric. Sew the short ends together, creating another tube. Turn the bag inside out. Sew the unhemmed edge of the fabric tube to the top edge of the cargo pants tube.

5. With the seam in the center back, sew with a clean finish across the bottom of the cargo tube, creating the general bag shape.

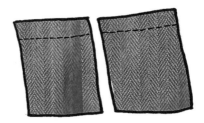

inside out view

6. Cutting around the zipper, cut a piece from the pants that is 5" x 9" (12.5cm x 23cm). Then cut out 2 rectangular pieces from the back bottom of the pants, including the cuffs, each 6½" x 9" (16.5cm x 23cm).

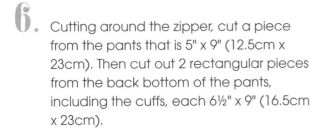

7. Cut the remaining piece of the waistband off of the pants and cut 2 pieces from it, each 7" (18cm) long.

8. Sew each 9"- (23cm-) long side of the zipper piece to a 9" (23cm) side of a rectangle from the back bottom of the pants with a clean finish; the zipper piece should be centered between the 2 rectangles. This creates the front flap for the bag.

9. Place 1 of the pieces cut off from the waistband vertically along the center of each rectangle (excluding the zipper piece). Sew them on, as shown, creating 2 parallel loops through which you will thread the bag strap (so make sure to reinforce the loops!), leaving the edges raw.

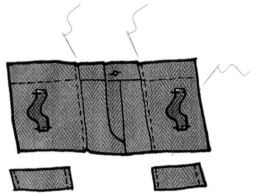

10. Cut another piece of the scrap fabric the same size as the front flap piece. **Make 2 buttonholes**, each 2" (5cm) from the short sides and 3" (7.5cm) from the top.

11. Sew the fabric to the back side of the front flap with a clean finish. Be sure to leave a small hole on the perimeter to facilitate turning the front piece right side out. Turn it right side out, then **hand-stitch** the small hole shut.

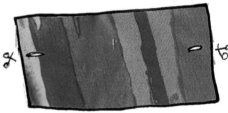

12. Push the scrap fabric tube at the top of the bag into the bag itself, so that it becomes a lining around the top rim of the bag. In at least 4 places at the bottom of the lining, tack the fabric with hand-stitches to the inside of the bag to secure it.

13. Sew the flap to the top of the bag back with a clean finish so that when the flap falls over the top of the bag, the button from the fly of the cargo pants is hanging in front.

14. **Sew 2 buttons** onto the front piece of the bag where shown, placing them to match up with the buttonholes in the fabric piece. This is the closure for the bag, so make sure the buttons are secure.

15. Using the remaining fabric from the scrap and the pants, cut enough strips to sew together 1 long scrap fabric strip and 1 long cargo strip, each 70" (178cm) long and 3" (7.5cm) wide. Sew the short ends of the fabric pieces together to create the long fabric strip, then sew the short ends of the cargo pieces together to create the long cargo strip.

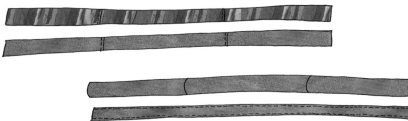

16. Sew the 2 long strips on top of each other with a clean finish to create a long, thin, tube. After turning the tube, iron it flat and **topstitch** the 2 long sides to flatten the tube completely. Place the strip through the 2 loops on the front piece, and sew the short ends of the strip together to create a large handle.

Military bags have been in vogue for decades, but often they look drab and déjà vu. The Cargo Carry-All adds new pizzazz to this old time favorite. Its military fatigue origins make it versatile, durable, and über-utilitarian, while the fun lining fabric kicks boring to the curb.

QUICK TIP: Turn this bag into the perfect laptop carrier by lining it with 2 layers of bubble wrap. You will need four 4" x 13" x 6" (10cm x 33cm x 15cm) rectangles of bubble wrap. Turn the bag inside out and place 2 rectangles on the inside, front of the bag (underneath the inside top trim). Stitch in place on the edges and corners to secure. Repeat with the inside back of bag.

FUN FACT: Did you know that the Carabinieri (Italian Police) uniform was designed by Giorgio Armani? Oh, those stylish Italians!

SWEATER COMPUTER COZY

YOU'LL NEED

- 1 old wool sweater
- 3 yards (2.7m) yarn
- 1 zipper, about 20" (51cm) long
- Pins

DIMENSIONS

16" x 10" (32cm x 25.5cm)

1. Wash your wool sweater on hot so that it shrinks and "felts." Dry your sweater.

2. If your sweater has a zipper or buttons that open the sweater in front, cut them off. If it does not, cut the front of the sweater open anyway.

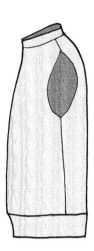

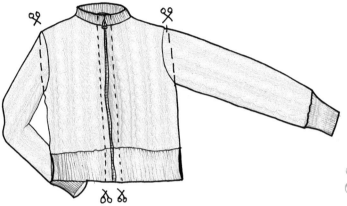

3. Cut the sleeves of the sweater off.

4. Stitch both armholes closed.

5. As shown, fold the sweater on its side so that 1 of the stitched armholes lies center-front. Place your laptop computer onto the sweater. Mark the length of the computer with pins on the sweater. Cut the collar and the bottom off of the sweater so that the remaining piece is ½" (13mm) longer than the computer on each side.

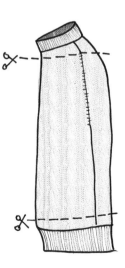

PULLOVER PROCESSOR

We all have mini fashion disasters—buttons falling off of coats, stains, and worst of all, shrinking that fave old sweater in the wash. At the Compai Compound, we have learned to see these mishaps as windows of opportunity. So the next time your favorite wool sweater ends up in the wash, don't use it to clean your bathroom floor—hook your computer up with a new winter wardrobe!

QUICK TIP: Make sure the sweater is made of at least 80 percent animal fiber (wool, alpaca, cashmere—you know, the good stuff), or it won't felt. Then machine wash your sweater in hot water and dry it on hot in the dryer.

FUN FACT: Did you know that March 20 is National Sweater Day? Yes folks, now your computer can celebrate with the rest of us!

6. Sew the top edges of the bag together with a **clean finish**.

7. **Pin** the zipper onto the open edge of the case, wrapping it around the open corner of the sweater. Stitch the zipper into place and then **whipstitch** any remaining openings closed if the zipper doesn't reach the bottom corner of the case.

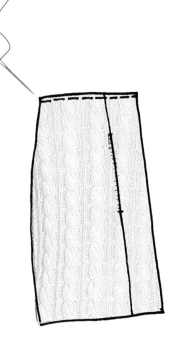

8. The pom-poms on our design were originally part of the sweater that we used, but if you'd like to add pom-poms to your design, wrap the yarn in a figure 8 around your index finger and thumb, in small loops, about 70 times. Pull the looped figure 8 off your fingers, then wrap the yarn around the center of those loops several times, tie a knot. Cut the loops open and throw the pom-pom in the dryer. When the dry cycle is complete, tie the pom-pom to the hole in the zipper pull.

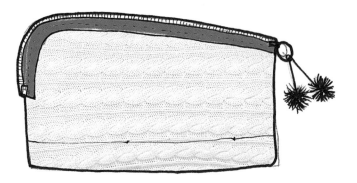

UGLY ORIGINAL {designer feature}

"Be the ugly original, not a beautiful imitation."—Yehuda Safran

Herein lies the inspiration behind Jae H. Kim's contemporary bag creations. Kim believes that the value of originality can outweigh the importance of conventional (and often not so original) beauty.

Kim works with materials he finds on his weekly adventures to secondhand stores, hardware stores, and on the streets of Brooklyn. He says, "The stories in the old materials make things unique." His impeccably hand-crafted creations embody the perfect balance between the old and the new. He uses old canvas, for example, and then paints it with latex, which not only gives it a very matte, industrial feel but also waterproofs the material. Next, he personalizes the bags with found charms and trinkets. It is this sort of ingenuity that sets Kim apart in his realm.

One of the keys to Kim's success is that he is never afraid to ask questions, and he has learned many useful techniques and tricks of the trade this way. You don't know something? Ask someone who might. And if no one has the answer, Kim suggests this: "Interact with the material. Try to have a conversation with it."

Name
Jae H. Kim

Company
Ugly Original

Occupation
Fashion Designer

Age
30

Location
Williamsburg,
New York

Bag Description
Canvas utility bag
made from an "A" tent,
painted with latex and
decorated with vintage
accoutrements

Inspiration
1960s military aviator
kit bags, time, and old
things

✚ Kim uses latex paint to waterproof the bottom of his bags for an industrial look and durability. Try painting the bottom of one of your utility bags, such as the backpack, with latex paint to make it even more utilitarian!

✚ How many times have you been stifled by doubt during the creative process? Kim believes that this is precisely the moment when you should persevere. You may be on the brink of creating something grand! Kim should know; his stunning "ugly originals" sell in the hippest boutiques in NYC for top dollar.

SUIT MESSENGER BAG

YOU'LL NEED

- 1 old suit jacket
- 1 pair khaki pants
- Pins

DIMENSIONS

17" x 14" x 5" (43cm x 35.5cm x 12.5 cm)

1. Cut the jacket off horizontally, 15" (38cm) up from the bottom edge, all the way around.

2. Cut 1 sleeve off 10" (25.5cm) from the cuff.

3. Lay the cut jacket piece flat and cut out the middle section, leaving you with 2 equal-sized pieces, each 16" (40.5cm) wide (depending on the size of the jacket that you started out with.)

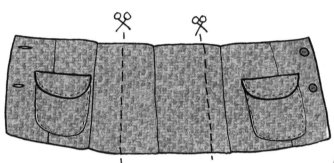

4. Cut a hole in the pocket on the piece with the buttons, as shown, and stitch the pocket closed on the open end, sewing the flap down if your pocket has one.

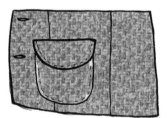
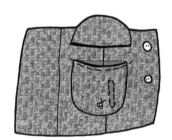

5. Sew the 2 pieces of the jacket with pockets together with a **clean finish** at the raw ends, and fold in half.

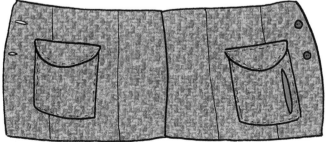

6. Cut the waistband off the pants. Cut out an arched shape, 16" (40.5cm) tall and 6" (15cm) wide, from the front and back of one pant leg, as shown.

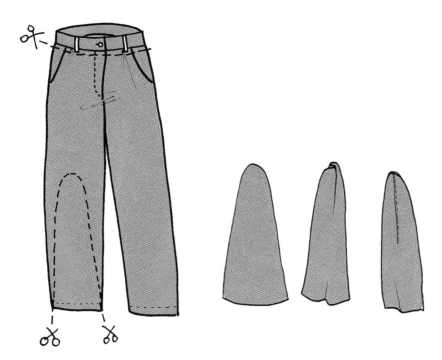

7. Fold the middle of the rounded edge of one arched shape and sew to create a 9" (23cm) **dart**. Repeat with the other arched shape.

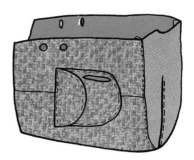

8. Sew the arched shapes inside the folded edges of the suit jacket bottom with a clean finish, as shown.

9. Cut a 6"- (15cm-) long oval around the buttons on the sleeve piece cut off in step 2 (if there are no buttons, just cut where they would be). **Roll hem** the edges of the oval.

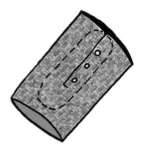

10. Cut the waistband in half widthwise. Sew along long edges of both pieces of the waistband to reattach any loose belt loops.

11. Sew the short ends of the oval to the raw edges of the waistband, as shown, creating the handle for the bag's strap.

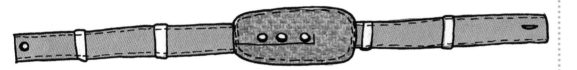

12. Place 1 end of the strap against an inner side of the bag, folding the inner edges of the side to overlap the strap (as shown in illustration). Make sure that at least 3½" (9cm) of the strap overlaps the side edge for strength. **Hand-stitch** into place, sewing back and forth several times to ensure that the handle is sturdy.

13. Cut a 2½" x 14" (6.5cm x 35.5cm) strip from the pants and **hem** both sides of the strip. **Pin** the hemmed strip around the hole that was cut into the pocket in step 4, and use the strip to sew a **covered hem** around the pocket hole, to finish the edges of the hole.

14. Add decorative **whipstitches** around the pocket flap or anywhere else to add a vintage flair.

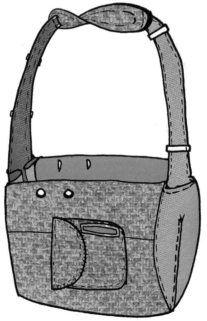

TWEED TRAVELER

After a while, recycling becomes second nature. When we see a suit jacket with a great lining or a fun detail on the pockets or lapels, we automatically begin to think how that detail could fit onto a bag. On this suit jacket, our favorite details were the leather buttons, so we made sure to put them in a prominent position in our design.

QUICK TIP: This bag looks great with added hand-sewn details—check out our whipstitch around the mouth of the pocket. But don't limit yourself to what you see in this book! The only limit on your creativity is your own imagination.

RECYCLE IT: Just can't bring yourself to cut up your beloved suit? Donate it to an organization like Dress for Success (dressforsuccess.org), which provides business attire for underprivileged people seeking employment.

DAPPER DIAPER BAG

YOU'LL NEED

- 1 old quilted blanket
- 50" (127cm) elastic
- Pins

DIMENSIONS

19" x 16" x 7" (48.5cm x 40.5cm x 18cm)

1. Cut out two 21" x 14" (53.5cm x 35.5cm) rectangles from the quilt. Round off 2 corners of 1 long edge on each rectangle as shown, approximately 2½" x 2" (6.5cm x 5cm).

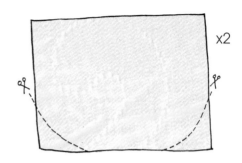

2. Cut out 1 long 9" x 52" (23cm x 132cm) strip from the quilt, preserving the edges for step 8. Cut out small squares and rectangles for pockets, using your imagination for sizing. Do you want to fit a bottle on the outside? Then make the pocket about 5" x 7" (12.5cm x 18cm). Do you want a pocket for a pacifier or diapers? Cut the pocket piece accordingly. **Hem** each pocket piece, then stitch the pockets onto the ends of the strip at least 1½" (3.8cm) apart and 1½" (3.8cm) from the top of the strip, remembering to leave the pocket openings facing outward, as shown.

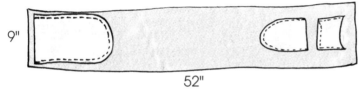

9"

52"

3. Cut a 16" x 7" (40.5 x 18cm) rectangle for the large front pocket. Hem all edges of the rectangle. Cut a 10" (25.5cm) length of elastic and sew it onto 1 of the 16" (40.5cm) edges with a **zigzag stitch**, stretching the elastic to fit the edge you sew. This will **gather** the top edge of the pocket. Stitch the 3 nongathered edges of the pocket to the center of 1 of the rounded rectangles cut out in step 1.

4. **Pin** the long strip to the edges of the rounded rectangles and sew them together with a **clean finish**, as shown.

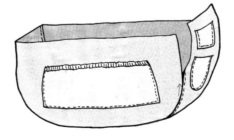

SECURITY BLANKET

Old quilts are the best, the sort of thing you want to pass on to your kids and grandkids. But what do you do when your quilt starts to look like a shabby rag? Salvage it by using the part that is still intact to make a diaper bag, and then pass that on from generation to generation. Tradition meets innovation.

QUICK TIP: Diaper bags are all about practicality. Make yours to suit your needs. We made ours with a side pocket for easy access to the baby bottle; you may want insulate a bottle pocket with fiberfill to keep the bottle warm or cold.

RECYCLE IT: If your quilt is big and you only used a portion of it to make your bag, cut out a 3' x 4' (91cm x 122cm) square, sew a wide covered hem around the edge, and it's a perfect little matching baby blanket!

5. Using a zig-zag stitch, sew the remaining 40" (101.5cm) length of elastic to the top edge of the bag, stretching the elastic as you sew to gather the fabric.

6. Cut a 4" x 30" (10cm x 76cm) strip of the quilt. Hem the long edges of the strip and sew the 2 short ends together, creating a loop.

7. Fold the loop lengthwise over the top edge of the bag, pinning as you go. Sew the loop in place as a **covered hem**.

8. Cut two 20" x 5" (51cm x 12.5cm) strips from the edge of the quilt. **Roll hem** the raw edges of the strips. Sew the ends of the strips to the bag 3" (7.5 cm) from the side seams, 1 in the center front, and 1 in the center back, with a clean finish, to create 2 handles.

STEPHANIE ARPAGE {designer feature}

Stephanie Arpage was born in the hills of Aix-en-Provence, France. Some of her fondest childhood memories are of rummaging through the attic of her family home amid overflowing trunks of antique jewelry, high-heeled shoes, and precious antique fabrics. Foraging both indoors and out, inspired her.

"Initially, I discovered my self-expression through sketching and dedicated my creative soul to visual arts. Through painting, photography, and video, I take a closer look at the human body: I study the curves, the tensions, the anatomy, the imperfections, whatever changes the ordinary into extraordinary." Arpage's creations reflect her interest in the body by being practical and ergonomic, but they are also true to her own whimsical, romantic, and oh-so-French spirit. "My collection is dedicated to free-spirited, mysterious women, women who are particularly demanding about the ways they lead their life." Women a lot like herself.

Name
Stephanie Arpage

URL
stephaniearpage.com

Occupation
Indie Designer, Visual Artist, Mom

Age
32

Location
Williamsburg, New York

Bag Description
A chic everyday bag made from a vintage curtain and leather from an old vest, complete with an adjustable strap made from the vest's zipper

➕ Part of the genius of Arpage's creations lies in the balance of practical form and playful style. To achieve this in your own designs, study your everyday bag. What makes it the bag you always use? Its shape? The way it conforms to your body? Use this knowledge as you create the bags in this book to better suit them to your own, individual body.

➕ We love the "fin" that Arpage sewed into the seam of this bag. If you like the look too, why not add a fin to an existing handbag? Just add pleats to a leather remnant and sew it to the bag.

CHAPTER 3

SHOPPERS & TOTES

Totes and shoppers are all the rage these days. Who wants to be seen carrying a disposable bag? We are finally beginning to realize that we cannot continue to use paper and plastic bags every time we shop. In response to this, many stores now sell reusable totes that help save the planet while conveying the message "I care about our earth." Well, what if instead of buying one you made that tote yourself from recycled materials? What if that tote was actually cute (unlike many of the premade shoppers out there)? This chapter will show you how to make a lightweight, waterproof tote from an umbrella (**Rainy Day Shopper**), a hot beach tote from your favorite towel (**Towel-It Tote**), and even a farmers market–ready shopper from a coffee sack (**Burlap Shopper**). These bags, if they could speak, would say, "Not only do I care about this earth, but I have mad style and mad skillz."

BURLAP SHOPPER PG. 52

BURLAP SHOPPER

YOU'LL NEED

- 1 burlap sack (a coffee sack works well)

- 40" x 26" (101.5cm x 66cm) scrap of fabric

- Vintage button

- An old sash, at least 64" (163cm) long

- 18" x 7" (45.5cm x 18cm) piece of cardboard

DIMENSIONS

17" x 20" x 7" (43cm x 51cm x 18cm)

1. Cut 2 identical 10" x 24" (25.5cm x 61cm) rectangles from the burlap sack.

2. Cut two 8½" x 24" (21.5cm x 61cm) rectangles from the scrap fabric, pieces (**A**) and (**B**). Next, cut four 5" x 26" (12.5cm x 66cm) rectangles from the scrap fabric, pairs (**C**) and (**D**).

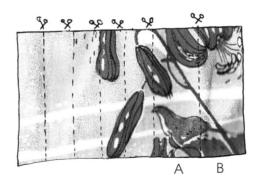

A   B

3. Round off the 2 top corners on (**C**) and (**D**) as shown, approximately 1½" x1½" (3.8cm x 3.8cm).

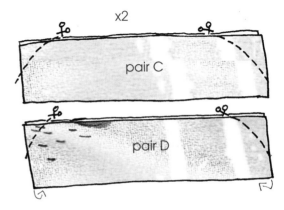

x2

pair C

pair D

4. Sew pair (**C**) together on 3 sides with a **clean finish**, leaving the straight, bottom edge open. Repeat with pair (**D**). Fold the bottom edge in 1" (2.5cm) and iron flat on both pairs.

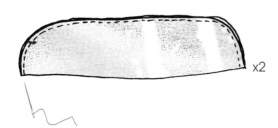

x2

5. Sew the 24" (61cm) sides of 1 burlap rectangle (cut out in step 1) and rectangle (**A**) (cut out in step 2) together. Repeat with the remaining burlap piece and piece (**B**), creating pieces (**E**) and (**F**).

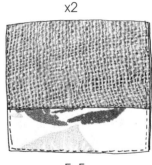

x2

E, F

6. From the remaining scrap fabric, cut out a 10" x 10" (25.5cm x 25.5 cm) square for the pocket. Round the edges of 2 of the corners of the square as shown, 1½" x 1½" (3.8cm x 3.8cm), then cut tiny vertical slits into the fabric where it was rounded to facilitate the **curved seam**. **Hem** all 4 sides of the rectangle.

7. **Pin** and stitch the bottom and sides of the small rectangle to the center of piece (**E**), 3" (7.5cm) from the top of the burlap, to create a pocket.

8. Cut a strip of fabric 1" (2.5cm) wide and 4" (10cm) long. Hem the sides of the strip and sew both ends of it to the top center of the burlap piece that has the pocket, creating a loop on the front of the piece, as shown.

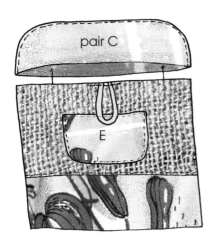
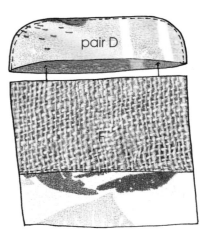

9. Insert piece (**E**) 1" (2.5cm) into the opening in pair (**C**) , and **topstitch** closed. Repeat by inserting piece (**F**) into pair (**D**), as shown, creating the front and back pieces of the bag.

10. Sew the 2 large pieces together (right sides facing) on the 2 sides and bottom with a clean finish, leaving the top rounded edges open, to create the general shape of the bag.

11. With the bag still inside out, pinch the bottom corner so that it creates a triangle 2½" (6.5cm) long, pull the tip of the triangle upward, and sew a line across the tip to fix the triangle into place. Repeat this step on the other bottom corner. This will create a "bottom" for the bag that didn't exist before.

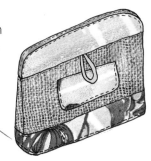

12. Topstitch around the new bottom of the bag to define the shape. Cut a piece of cardboard the same size as the new bottom of the bag, and using a stapler, cover the cardboard in fabric. Place the fabric-covered cardboard on the bottom inside the bag.

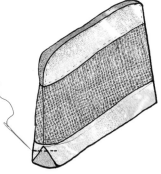

inside view

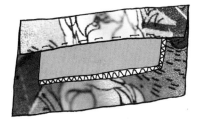

13. Cut the sash in half widthwise and hem any raw edges. Stitch the sash to the front and the back of the bag, as shown, to create handles. Be sure that the sash is evenly placed, about 5" (12.5cm) from the edges, so the bag is level when carried.

A-TISKET A-TASKET

I am sure you've seen it before . . . that black-and-white image of a beautiful young European woman at an outdoor market with a woven basket, buying flowers and a baguette . . . *a basket??* Come on!! Cute, but who in their right mind would use a basket to shop these days? Luckily, with the Burlap Shopper, you can have it all—the practicality of a shopper (it even has a little front pocket for your keys!) and the romantic aesthetics of *le marche' a Paris*!

QUICK TIP: Don't know where to find a burlap bag? In general, burlap bags are used for transporting coffee beans, potatoes, and grain (such as rice)—try your local Asian market or online sites such as recycle.net.

FUN FACT: Did you know that burlap is made from jute? I know what you're thinking—what the heck is that? Well, it's a natural vegetable fiber. What could be better suited to carry your vegetables, n'est–ce pas?

YOU'LL NEED

- 1 broken umbrella
- 1 lightweight button

DIMENSIONS

27" x 17" (69cm x 43cm)

*The Rainy Day Shopper is three bags in one. Wear it open or closed, or wrap it up and stash it in your purse for eco-licious grocery shopping.

1. Carefully remove the umbrella fabric from its metal skeleton.

2. Fold the umbrella fabric in half and cut off 1 panel on each side of the fabric, in front and in back, so that you are left with 2 identical pointed pieces, as shown. Be sure not to cut off the panel containing the little Velcro strap that holds the umbrella closed. Put the remaining fabric aside, as we will need it later.

3. Measure 6" (15cm) down from the top point of the pointed pieces, and cut off the tip of both pieces.

4. Sew the 2 pointed pieces together with a **clean finish** along the perimeter, leaving the sides that used to be the bottom edge of the umbrella open.

5. From the remnants cut off in step 2, cut 2 strips of fabric, each 12" x 3" (30.5cm x 7.5cm).

6. Fold each strip in half lengthwise, right side in. Sew the long edge closed. Using a safety pin, turn the tubes right side out.

UMBRELLA UNLIMITED

In the winter, gutters are littered with broken umbrellas. Umbrellas are fragile creatures . . . they flip inside out, they cease to open or close, or their skeletons snap. But fear not; the umbrella is reborn as a true eco-tote. Not only is it constructed from a broken umbrella diverted from overflowing landfills, but it folds up to be carried around at all times. Utilize this clever carryall instead of our least favorite bag: the plastic one.

QUICK TIP: One umbrella contains enough fabric to make 2 bags! So hook yourself up with a bit of Velcro and make a bag for your mom, too!

RECYCLE IT: Don't throw out the umbrella's skeleton after you've removed the fabric from it. Hang the skeleton in your laundry room or shower as a handy drying rack for your lingerie! Air-drying your clothes conserves 3–4 kilowatt hours per load of laundry.

7. Position the ends of a tube about 3" (7.5cm) from the tip. Stitch one end of this tube onto each side of the tip of the fabric to create the first handle. Sew back and forth several times to make sure the handle is secure. Repeat this process with the remaining tube on the opposite side of the top of the bag.

8. Cut an 8" x 10" (20.5cm x 25.5cm) rectangle from the umbrella remnants. Fold the rectangle in half widthwise and sew the sides closed with a clean finish to create a small pouch.

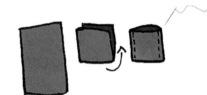

9. Cut a 2" x 1" (5cm x 2.5cm) strip from the scrap fabric. Fold the fabric in thirds, lengthwise, creating a very narrow strip. Stitch the ends of the strip together, forming a loop, and then stitch the strip to the inside center, top of the pouch. Make sure the loop is big enough to fit the button through.

10. **Sew the button** to the opposite side of the pouch in a corresponding location to the loop.

11. Sew the pouch along the inside top edge onto the upper, left corner of the bag. You can now stuff the entire bag into the little pouch and pop it into your purse for impromptu shopping trips!

PRIX PRIX {designer feature}

Laura Skelton's designs are "bold, without going over the top." She attributes her clean-lined design aesthetic to her background in architecture. Skelton's mother taught her to sew when she was a kid, but it wasn't until a high school summer program that she began reconstructing vintage materials to create new designs. "I used lots of T-shirts and remade them with knots and safety pins. My first recycled bag was made from a pair of blue jeans using very basic sewing techniques. If I saw something I liked, I would come home and try to make it myself," says Skelton. This go-getter attitude has served Skelton well; her company Prix-Prix now sells recycled wares all over the world. We know a thing or two about running an indie design company ourselves and find, as Skelton demonstrates, that it's all about being resourceful and innovative: "I never let the fact that I have not done something before stop me from trying to figure it out and playing around with ideas."

A secret of Skelton's success? "I make wallets that are great for men, who are underserved in the indie design community, and they reward me by buying them up!"

Aside from thrift shops and rummage sales, Skelton finds materials on **Freecycle.org,** an organization through which neighbors give away things they no longer use. She also takes advantage of Etsy.com for large quantities of inexpensive vintage clothing and materials for reuse.

Name
Laura Skelton

URL
prix-prix.com

Occupation
Indie Designer

Age
24

Location
New Orleans, Louisiana

Bag Description
"The Overnighter" is a shoulder bag made from a children's sleeping bag

Key Techniques
Sewing and turning a tube, slipstitch, and re-appropriating an object's materials: the fabric, zipper closure, and lining are all from the sleeping bag

BOHO HOBO BAG

YOU'LL NEED

- One A-line skirt
- A vintage closure (try a toggle closure, or even 2 ribbons to tie together)
- Pins

DIMENSIONS

24" x 15" (61cm x 38cm)

1. Cut out 2 equal-sized parallelograms, each 30" x 23" x 36" (76cm x 58.5cm x 91cm), from the bottom of the skirt.

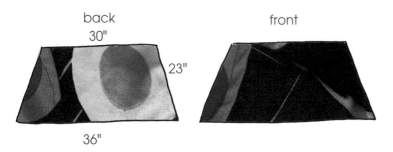

back
30"
23"
36"
front

2. Create a 2"- (5cm-) deep vertical fold perpendicular to the center bottom hemline of the back piece. **Pin** to secure the fold in place, creating a **tuck**. Sew across the bottom, securing the tuck into place. Next, create two, 1"- (2.5cm-) deep vertical folds, each 10" (25.5cm) from the ends of the front piece. Pin and sew both folds into place to create 2 more tucks.

back   front   back   front

3. Place the front and back pieces together, right sides in, and sew along the sides and bottom edges with a **clean finish**. On the top of the bag, cut out what will become the handles, as shown. Each handle should be 6" (15cm) long and 12" (30.5cm) apart in the front and back.

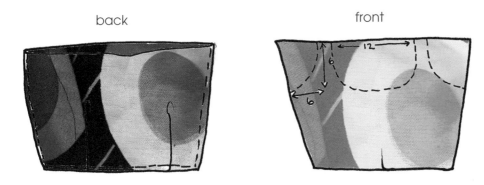

back   front

4. Cut out tiny triangles around the top edges of the bag, and then sew a **curved seam,** as shown.

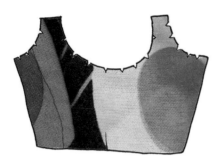 

5. Sew the top edges of the handles on each side of the bag togther with a clean finish. Then, 2" (5cm) from the top, sew a straight line across each handle, catching both sides of the handle to create a small loop at the top of each handle.

6. Cut out a half circle 16" (40.5cm) wide and 8" (20.5cm) tall for the front flap. Create a 1" (2.5cm) deep vertical fold in the center of the straight edge of the half circle. Pin into place. Cut small triangles around the rounded edged of the semicircle. **Roll hem** the edges, securing the tuck into place.

 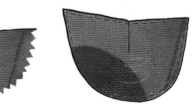

7. Cut out a 36" x 7" (91cm x 18cm) rectangle from the skirt fabric. Fold the fabric in half lengthwise, right side in, and sew along the long edge, with a clean finish, creating a tube. Turn the tube right side out.

8. Tie a knot at 1 end of the tube and feed the loose end through the first handle loop. Thread it through the second loop and tie another knot to secure the loose end of the handle in place.

9. Now sew each half of the closure onto corresponding locations at the front center of your new bag and flap.

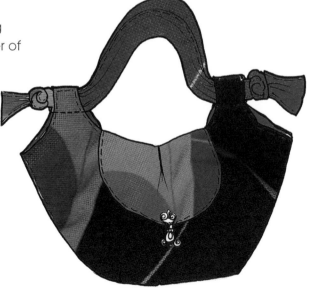

DAY TRIPPING

Your wallet and your keys, the snack, the book, the makeup, the water, those celebrity-size sunglasses . . . Somehow, there never seems to be enough room in a handbag. Fortunately, the Boho Hobo Bag is not just hip enough for a Soho stroll, it is deceptively spacious—just the right size for a day on the town.

QUICK TIPS: Quickly coordinate this bag with any outfit by swapping the fabric handle with a belt. Remove the fabric handle and thread the belt through the 2 handle loops on the bag. Then just buckle the belt. Ta-da! You can create as many new looks for this bag as you have belts in your closet.

RECYCLE IT: When choosing fabric for this project, look for a long, wide, 1970s-era skirt. It will have enough fabric that you'll be able to carve off the upper portion to create a matching mini.

TOWEL-IT TOTE

YOU'LL NEED

- 1 towel, at least 16" x 32" (40.5cm x 81cm)
- 1 rubber bath mat
- Parchment paper
- Pins

DIMENSIONS

13½" x 15" (34.5cm x 38cm)

1. Cut out a 14" x 30" (35.5cm x 76cm) rectangle from your towel.

2. Cut out 2 identical winged shapes from the rubber bath mat, 14" (35.5cm) wide and 6" (15cm) tall at the tallest point. The circular-shaped cutout in the center should be large enough to cup your hand around and the outer ring should be 6" (15cm) in diameter. The wings should extend out-ward from the ring shape about 2½" (6.5cm) on both sides.

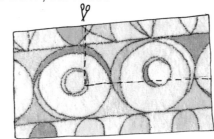

x2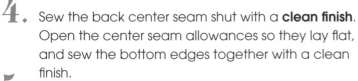

3. Fold the ends of the towel toward the center so they are touching. **Pin** together the 2 sides in the back and then pin together the bottom.

4. Sew the back center seam shut with a **clean finish**. Open the center seam allowances so they lay flat, and sew the bottom edges together with a clean finish.

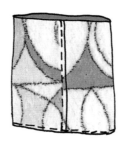

5. Pin 1 of the handles cut out in step 2 onto the top front of the bag (the side with no center seam). **Topstitch** the handle to the bag. Help the rubber glide into the machine by sewing with parchment paper sandwiched above and below the rubber.

6. Repeat on the back side of the bag with the other handle, making sure to line up the handles perfectly. Sew the side ends of the rubber handles together. Cut out the bit of towel that is visible through the hole in the handle.

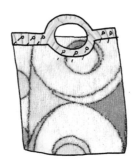

TERRY-ALL CARRYALL

In Italy we had a dear friend who worked for Pucci, you know, that famous Florentine fashion house known for its wild, graphic prints?! Well anyway, he gifted us the *super*-lux towel you see here. We couldn't help but feel that such a high-fashion fabric deserved a more prominent position in our wardrobe, so we transformed it into our latest fave accessory—big, glamorous oversized sunglasses required.

QUICK TIP: Stuck with plain Jane bath towels? Cut them into strips or squares and resew them together for a patchwork effect, or tie dye a light-colored towel to create your own cool print.

RECYCLE IT: Don't you throw away the rest of that bath mat! Come on, you can make another bag out of that. Check out the Bath Mat Bag-It project on page 16.

SHOWER CURTAIN TOTE

YOU'LL NEED

- 1 shower curtain

- 10" x 36" (25.5cm x 91cm) scrap of woven fabric

- Parchment paper

DIMENSIONS

14" x 14" (35.5cm x 35.5 cm)

1. Cut a 25" x 32" (63.5cm x 81cm) rectangle from the shower curtain. Fold the bottom of the rectangle upward 6" (15cm).

2. Fold the top of the rectangle down 5" (12.5cm).

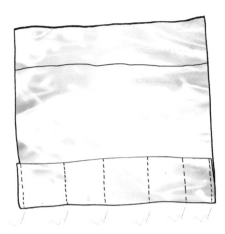

3. Place parchment paper over and under the folds and sew the folds down on both ends of the curtain. Every 6" (15cm) along the bottom of the curtain, sew a vertical seam to hold the fold into place and create 5 pockets. Whenever you sew over the curtain, place parchment paper over and under the plastic to help the sewing machine glide over the plastic. When the seam is in place, carefully rip the parchment paper off.

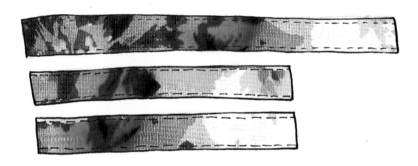

4. Cut 3 strips from the scrap fabric. The first should be 3" x 30" (7.5cm x 76cm); the second and third strips should 3" x 21" (7.5cm x 53.5cm). **Roll hem** all 3 strips on the long sides.

5. Place the longest strip 3" from the top folded edge of the bag. Use a couple pieces of tape to hold it in place, then cover the area with parchment paper on the bottom, and stitch the bottom edge of the strip onto the curtain.

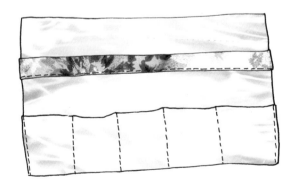

WET AND WILD

Picture this . . . you are at the beach, relaxing in the sun. You glance up at the horizon and spot him. You know, that dream boy from your favorite TV show? You think quick, and reach for your camera in your beach bag—your friends will never believe this! You scramble for your camera amid the chaos of your bag, and when you finally look up . . . he is gone. If only you had the transparent Shower Curtain Bag! With this see-through, pocketed wonder you'll never lose time (and the photo op of a lifetime) again.

QUICK TIP: Use a leather needle with your sewing machine for sewing the plastic. These heavyweight needles boast a razor tip perfect for piercing tough PVC.

Not So Fun Fact: Most shower curtains are made from polyvinyl chloride (PVC), a material that's notoriously hard to recycle. To make this tote work even harder, only buy a shower curtain that will eventually break down when you're done with it.

6. Fold the curtain in half widthwise and sew the sides together (using parchment paper) with a **clean finish**.

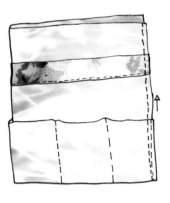

back view

7. Turn the bag so that the seam created in step 6, is in the center back of the bag. Sew the bottom of the bag (using parchment paper) with a clean finish.

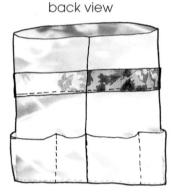

8. Place the ends of 1 of the shorter strips vertically under the top edge of the longer fabric strip to create the handle. Each end should be 3" (7.5cm) from the center of the bag. Repeat on the back with the remaining shorter strip. Sew all the way around the top edge of the longer strip, sewing the handles into place along the way.

GOSSIP GOSSIP {designer feature}

Jodi Bates has always been a serious DIY-er, but it was only after she got her hands on a big supply of discarded records that her design career took off. Inspired by the challenge of using recycled materials, Jodi found a way to make stylish handbags from the old records! "I long for a simpler time when production didn't create so much waste. Fashion that is fabulous one day can be on the curb in a matter of months. I've always felt that it's important to breath new life into old items—making them fun and fresh again—to reduce waste and explore creative boundaries."

When it comes to manufacturing, Jodi is a one-woman band, but she does rely on what she describes as "an amazing support team" to get everything done DIY style. "Everything about my company, Gossip Gossip, is DIY, from things as small as fabric labels to tags and fliers printed on 1920s letterpresses."

Jodi's sales are generally Internet based, and a large percentage are international (definitely one of the perks of doing online sales). She thanks sites like MySpace, Facebook, and Etsy for being a great source for networking and a huge support for kick-butt DIY-ers like herself!

Name
Jodi Bates

Company
Gossip Gossip

URL
myspace.com/gossipgossip

Occupation
Fashion Designer

Location
Portland, Oregon

Bag Description
Crafted with records, canvas, fabric, and strap webbing

Inspiration
Obsolete technology. "It amazes me that things which were around in my short lifetime are already considered a novelty (cassette tapes, beta, floppy disks, etc.). Seeing these items discarded inspires me to create something new from them."

✚ "Being true to fabricating items 100 percent DIY is time consuming and not always cost effective," Jodi says. "The first few years, I found it challenging to manage time and money in a way that was beneficial to my

DIY beliefs, but I stuck to it though!" And now Jodi is reaping the benefits of her creativity, vision, and perseverance. You can, too—that's what DIY is all about!

TARP SHOPPER

YOU'LL NEED

- 1 tarp, at least 30" x 30" (76cm x 76cm)
- 1 vintage button
- 4 plastic-bottle caps, 2 small and 2 large
- Pins

DIMENSIONS

17" x 17" (43cm x 43cm)

1. Cut out two 15" x 12" (38cm x 30.5cm) rectangles from the tarp. Place the pieces so that the right sides are facing out and the inside is facing in, and sew the bottom and 2 sides together with a **clean finish**, creating a pocket that will be the bottom portion of the bag.

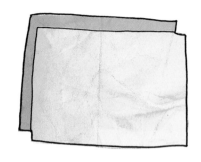

2. **Pleat** and **pin** the top edge of the pocket so the top rim of the bag is 16" (40.5cm) wide. Sew around the top rim of the pocket, sewing the gathers into place.

3. Cut two 9" x 6" (23cm x 15cm) rectangles from the tarp to create the top portion of the bag.

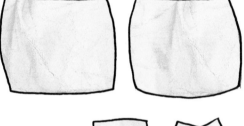

4. Cut out a smaller 3½" x 10½" (9cm x 26.5cm) rectangle from the tarp for the small front pocket. Round off 2 corners at 1 end, as shown. Pinch the opposite end at the center of the edge and create a ½"- (13mm-) deep fold. Sew the fold in place, creating a **dart**. This will allow the front pocket to have depth.

5. **Make a buttonhole** 1" (2.5cm) from the center of the rounded-corner end of the front pocket. Fold the pocket as shown. **Sew the button** onto the front pocket, beneath where the buttonhole falls when the flap closes.

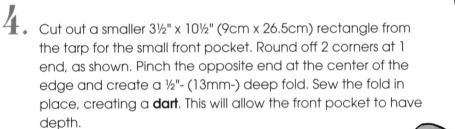

6. Stitch the front pocket, centered horizontally to 1 of the pieces cut out for the top of the bag in step 3. The bottom edge of the pocket should be stitched about 1" (2.5cm) from the bottom of the rectangle.

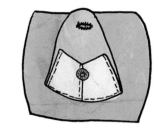
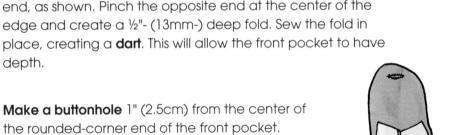

RUN FOR COVER

It is a rare moment when camping and fashion come together. But you know what? We at Compai believe recycling knows no boundaries—so we would like to present to you this ab-fab bag made out of an old tarp—perfect for a jaunt on a rainy day!

QUICK TIP: Tarps can be thick, so use a denim needle for sewing this bag. If working with a tarp proves too difficult, you can make this bag with a thick fabric instead. Then "plastify" the bottom with latex paint to make the fabric more "tarp-like."

FUN FACT: Tarp is short for tarpaulin— a word that supposedly originated on the docks, where sailors used tarred canvas to cover up things on their ship that they didn't want getting soaked. Eventually, people took to calling the sailors them- selves *tars*!

7. Place the rectangles for the top of the bag so that the right sides are facing out and the inside is facing in and sew the short sides together with a clean finish.

8. Turn the top and bottom portions of the bag inside out and sew the top and bottom portion of the bag to- gether with a clean finish, as shown, creating the body of the bag.

inside view

9. Cut out two 20" x 5" (51cm x 12.5cm) strips from the tarp. Fold the strips in half lengthwise.

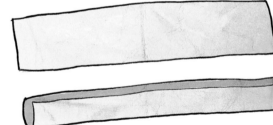

x2

10. Sew the long edges of each strip together with a clean finish, creating 2 long tubes.

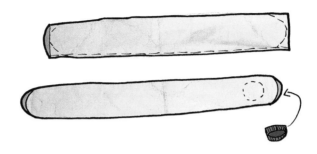

11. Lay the tubes down flat and cut off the corners into rounded ends on both strips.

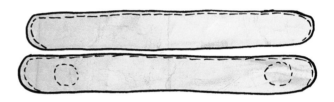

12. Place hot glue on the inside and outside of the larger bottle cap and carefully place it 2" (5cm) into the tube. (The inside of the cap should face out when the strap is attached.) Repeat with the other large bottle cap on the opposite end. Then **hand-stitch** the tubes closed, folding in the raw edges.

13. Stitch the ends of the handles just beneath the bottle caps to the top rim of the bag 2" (5cm) from the side edges, on the front and back. Place hot glue on the rims of the smaller bottle caps and push them into the fabric so that they fit inside the caps that are nestled inside the handles. Hold in place until dry.

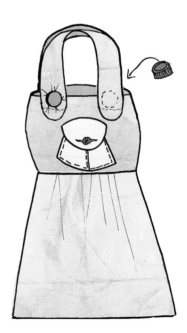

CHAPTER 4

SMALL BAGS & CLUTCHES

You don't have to be a savvy fashionista to know that a bag can make or break an outfit. (Try going to a gala with a backpack on if you don't believe me!) Special occasions require special bags; this is undeniable. This chapter is a virtual treasure chest of small bags and clutches. Precious little gems, these bags speak of class and style and will make you the centerpiece of any soiree. From the golden **Glitter-Much Clutch** made of paper fasteners (yes, ladies, we said paper fasteners—the ones floating at the bottom of your office drawer) to the groovy **Switch-It Suede Clutch** to the always topical **MagaBag** made from pages of your favorite magazines, these bags have the pizzazz to transform any outfit from occasional to special occasion.

MAGABAG PG. 96

PLASTIC BAG FUSION CLUTCH

YOU'LL NEED

- 3 black plastic bags, 3 tan plastic bags, and 6 white plastic bags

- 7" (18cm) zipper

- Parchment paper

- Brooch

- 5" x 5" (12.5cm x 12.5cm) piece of cardboard

- 30" x 5" (76cm x 12.5cm) ribbon

- Pins

DIMENSIONS

11" x 7" (28cm x 18cm)

1. In a well-ventilated area, turn on the iron (set it to rayon or a similar low temperature setting).

2. Cut the handles and bottoms off of all the bags, and then cut the bags open up the side so you are left with large rectangles.

3. Cut each rectangle in half so you are left with 24 pieces of plastic: 6 black, 6 tan, and 12 white.

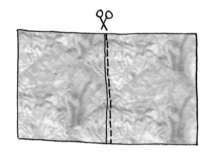

4. Lay parchment paper down on the ironing board. Then lay 6 white plastic squares down neatly on top of each other. (Attention! Do not put any printed ink on the top or the bottom of the pile, and don't face the printed pieces outward. The ink will come off.) Lay parchment paper on top of the plastic layers.

5. Iron the top, keeping the iron in constant motion, until the plastic is melted. Check periodically to be sure that iron is not so hot that it burns holes in the plastic and that all areas of the plastic, including the edges, are fusing together. Then flip the plastic over and iron the other side. Always use parchment paper between the iron and the plastic.

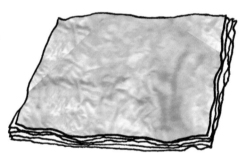

6. Repeat this process so you have 2 fused stacks of white bags, 1 stack of fused black bags, and 1 tan.

7. Cut out a 4" x 3" (10cm x 7.5cm) diamond shape from the cardboard using the utility knife. Each side should measure 2½" (6.5cm).

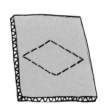

8. Use the cardboard diamond as a template to cut all of the fused plastic into diamonds. You'll need a total of 18 white diamonds, 12 tan diamonds, and 8 black diamonds, but cut out as many as you can to allow for error.

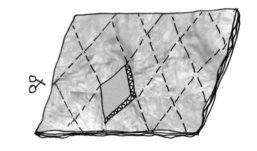

9. Sew 1 black diamond to 1 white diamond with a **clean finish**, attaching 1 side to another as shown. Now sew a tan diamond onto the white diamond so they make a long parallelogram.

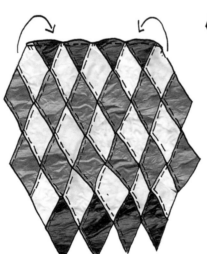

10. Continue systematically sewing the diamonds together in rows. Then, sew all the rows together to form the shown design.

11. Fold 1 row of black diamonds in half, creating a straight edge. Sew across this edge and then cut off the tips of the triangles. Repeat with the row of black diamonds at the opposite side of the shape.

12. Fold the plastic shape in half so that 2 black edges are aligned. Sew the sides closed.

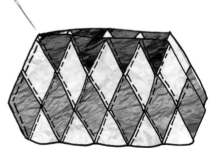

13. Turn the bag right side out. **Pin** the zipper in place along the top of the bag. Using a zipper foot, sew the zipper into the top opening of the bag.

14. Cut a 22" (56cm) length of ribbon. Sew the short ends together to create a tube. Fold the tube in half widthwise, then lengthwise, and iron flat. Insert the opening of the bag into the fold of the ribbon and **hand-stitch** the tube onto the top edge of the bag using a **whipstitch.**

15. Cut the ribbon into one 8" (20.5cm) length, and two 6" (15cm) lengths. Pin the long piece into a loop, and trim the ends of each short piece into forked shape, as shown. Pin a short piece centrally under the loop, and fold the other short piece into a "V." Pin this piece centrally under the loop as well, with the forked ends down. Take the remaining 2" (5cm) of ribbon, and wrap it perpendicularly around the center point of the loop, pinning in back. Sew a few stitches in the center, through all four ribbon pieces, and onto the bag to secure the bow. Remove the pins.

16. Pin a brooch onto the bow to add a touch of color, and voilà: trash to treasure!

EARTH FIRST PLASTIC PURSE

We hope that shortly after you acquire this precious guide to crafty bags you will never need to use a plastic bag again. But, just in case you happen to have a few lying around the house, the Plastic Bag Fusion Clutch is the perfect way to turn potential waste into a high fashion accessory!

QUICK TIP: Always monitor the temperature of the iron when fusing the bags. I won't name any names (Tina!), but *someone* burnt a hole in our first fusion bag creation. Consider yourself warned.

NOT SO FUN FACT: Plastic bags take more than 1,000 years to degrade in a landfill.

CERTAIN CURTAIN CLUTCH

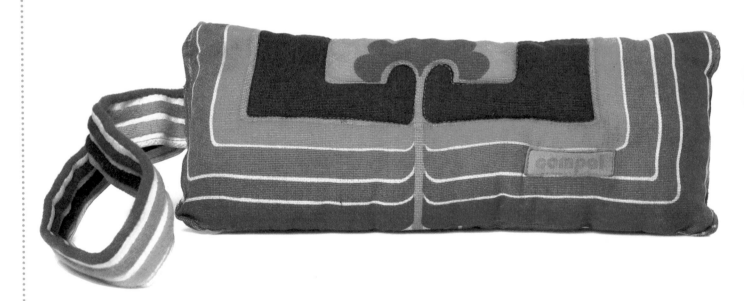

YOU'LL NEED

- 13" x 11" (33cm x 28cm) scrap from a curtain or other boldly printed fabric
- 1 fabric scrap of the same size for lining
- 11" (28cm) zipper
- 18" x 3" (45.5cm x 7.5cm) ribbon
- Something cushiony to use as filling; such as cotton or even scraps from an old sweater
- Pins

DIMENSIONS

10" x 4" (25.5cm x 10cm)

1. Place the curtain fabric face to face with the lining fabric. Sew around 3 sides, ¼" (6mm) from the edge, leaving one of the 11" (28cm) sides completely open.

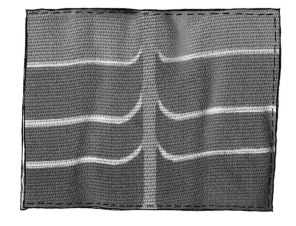

2. Turn the fabric right side out and evenly "stuff" your filling between the 2 pieces of fabric. Don't make the filling too thick, be sure to get the corners, and try to even the filling out as much as possible. **Pin** the filling in place.

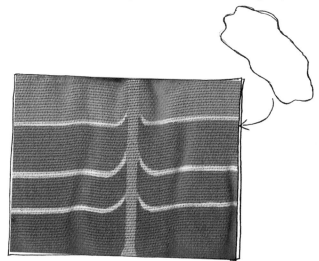

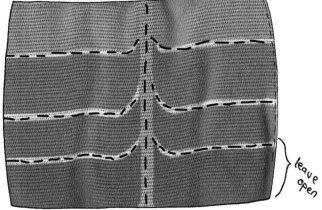

leave open

3. Fold the edges of the open side inward and **topstitch** it closed, leaving a 2¾" (7 cm) opening at one end.

4. We suggest using a contrasting thread color for this step. Choose a line on the bold pattern of the fabric that you'd like to follow. Being careful not to sew over the pins, slowly stitch over the line, following the pattern, **quilting** to secure the filling into place. Get as intricate as you'd like.

PADDED PLEASURE

Compai's very first collection was made of funky '70s curtains. We made skirts, tops, dresses, even hats—and of course, bags! The Certain Curtain Clutch is actually a Compai original from that first collection. We always have a blast working with curtains—it's like using yards of fabric, but with a recycling twist!

QUICK TIP: Do not, under any circumstances neglect to wash your curtain before making this bag—unless you want your clutch to double as a dust mite chateau!

RECYCLE IT: Little bag, lots of curtain? Stock up on filling and use the leftover fabric to make throw pillows! Just cut out a rectangle twice the desired length of your pillow. Fold the rectangle in half and sew the edges closed, leaving an opening through which to add the filling. Once you've stuffed the pillow, finish sewing the open edges together.

5. Once the quilting is complete, fold the ribbon in half lengthwise. Stitch the sides together as shown.

6. Fold the ribbon in half widthwise and place the ends 1" (2.5cm) from the top of the fabric inside the opening left in step 3. Sew the gap closed, catching the ribbon ends in the stitching.

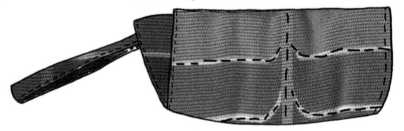

7. Fold the fabric in half lengthwise, and carefully topstitch the sides together, sewing slowly over the ribbon where the fabric is extra thick to avoid breaking the needle.

8. Sew the zipper into the top opening of the clutch with a **clean finish**.

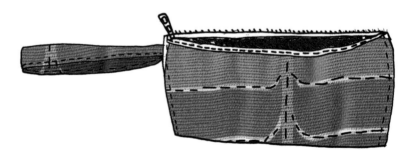

JOSH JAKUS {designer feature}

Josh Jakus got his training in architecture, and it shows. His designs are rigorous, modern, and essential. Jakus explains that his bag collection, called UM, developed from two creative challenges: "First, to make use of the unique properties of pressed wool felt, and second, to transform a flat surface into a volume using only the simplest of operations."

Why the name UM? Jakus recounts that a professor at UC Berkeley called his ingenius bag creations "Feltums," but he didn't like the name at all, so he simplified it to UM. Jakus is a master in simplification and utility. All of his bags unzip to lay flat for easy storage and cleaning.

"As far as the business side of things, I've had to learn through trial and error as I went along," explains Jakus. "The success of my work led me into business, and I had no idea what I was doing, but now, three years later, I feel like I earned an MBA through my experiences. The bad thing about doing it that way is that I've suffered through some bad business decisions, and I don't earn as much money as I could. But the good side is that I've been able to stay true to my core design principles, and this is priceless."

+ Jakus suggests first thinking of creating as a hobby and not as a potential business. "Product design was a hobby for me for five years, and then it only turned into a business when one of my designs got a lot of exposure. The competition is intense, and I think you have to do it for fun, and then if something comes of it, it's a bonus."

♻ If you do decide to take the leap into making a business from your recycled creations, take a cue from Jakus and consider using industrial excess. Factories create tons of waste that can be transformed into all kinds of accessories with a little imagination and a lot of ingenuity.

Name
Josh Jakus

URL
joshjakus.com

Occupation
Product Designer

Location
Berkeley, California

Bag Description
Bag made of industrial wool felt from factory excess

Inspiration
Making experiential connections between form and function

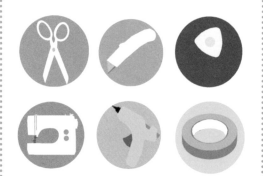

YOU'LL NEED

- 1 pair of old suede pants or an old suede jacket

- 2 round electrical plug plates

DIMENSIONS

8" x 6" (20.5cm x 15cm)

1. Cut a flat 20" x 30" (51cm x 76cm) piece of suede fabric from the suede clothing item. (We used an opened up leg piece from an old pair of suede pants to get that nifty preexisting seam down the center of the bag.) If your clothing item has a lining, remove it.

2. Cut about 20 long strips of suede from your clothing item, as long as possible and about ½" (3.8cm) wide.

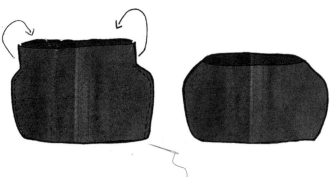

3. Fold the large piece of fabric in half lengthwise.

4. Draw the shape shown below, approximately 2" (5cm) high and 1½" (3.8cm) wide, with tailor's chalk on the sides of the fabric. Cut along the line, in front and back.

5. Turn the suede inside out, and sew the sides together with a **clean finish,** leaving 1" (2.5cm) open at the top of both sides.

6. Turn the bag right side out. Fold the top edges of the bag down inside the bag at the corners made in step 4. Glue the top part down to the inside of the bag so that the top rim of the bag has a clean, folded edge.

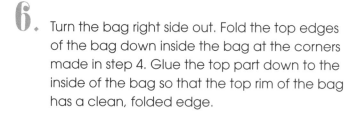

7. Place the first plug plate at the top center of the bag with the plug holes above the top edge of the bag. Using the chalk, outline the placement of the plate on the suede. Repeat on the bag back with the remaining plug plate.

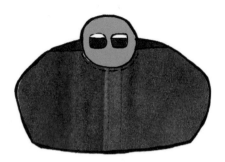

8. Use the craft knife to carefully make ½"- (13mm) slits in the suede creating a perforated line along the chalked arch to weave the suede strips into. Repeat on the bag back.

9. Place the plug plate directly above the slits as shown.

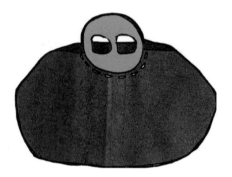

10. Wrap masking tape tightly around the end of the first strip of suede, like a shoelace. Tie a tight knot at the other end.

11. Push the tip of the strip through the back of the uppermost slit on the bag front; when the knot reaches the slit, place a dollop of hot glue between the knot and the slit to secure it in place.

12. Place the tip of the strip through the nearest hole in the plug plate and then back down and out through the next slit in the bag. Continue this process until the bottom of the plate is completely covered by suede strips.

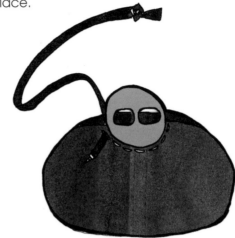

13. Now cover the upper part of the plate with suede strips, threading them though a slit and then up and over the plate and back into the slit. Dollop hot glue where needed to keep the strips in place.

14. If there are still portions of the plug plate uncovered, cut smaller pieces from the strips and glue them where needed. Be sure to cover any knots by gluing flat pieces of suede on top of them. Repeat steps 9–14 on the other bag back.

PLUGGED-IN PURSE

What do you get when you cross an electrical plug with a pair of old pants? It may sound like the beginning of a dirty joke, but this simple clutch will light up any girl's wardrobe. So grab some sharp scissors and rustle up an old pair of suede pants; they're destined for the slaughterhouse. Those pants may have been long out of style, but this bag is bound to become a timeless accessory.

QUICK TIP: Switch it up and use a square plug plate instead of a round one. Just take extra care to cover the sharp corners with the suede strips so that they don't slip from the plug plate.

RECYCLE IT: Suede can be an expensive second-hand commodity, so don't waste those scraps. Leftover suede makes great covers for journals. Use a hot glue gun to instantly transform a boring notebook into a matching accessory.

FOXY BOX BAG

YOU'LL NEED

- 1 cardboard cake mix box, about 8" x 6" (20.5cm x 15cm)

- 1 drawer pull (from an old dresser or a hardware store)

- 1 yard (91cm) woven fabric

- 2 small hinges

- Pins

- 12" x 6" (30.5cm x 15cm) cardboard

- Bottle cap

DIMENSIONS

8" x 6" (20.5cm x 15cm)

1. Cut a rectangle-shaped hole into 1 of the long sides of the box, leaving at least ¾" (2cm) of board on all sides (but make sure that the hole is large enough to stick your hand in . . . if it isn't, you'll need a larger box for this project.)

2. Measure the side of the box with the hole in it, and cut a rectangle from the additional piece of cardboard using those measurements for the lid.

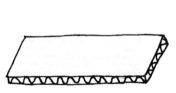

3. Tape up the rest of the box with masking tape to make it sturdy, sealing all the sides shut.

4. Cut a piece of fabric from the scrap fabric, 1½ times the length of the cardboard rectangle and twice the width.

5. Wrap the cardboard rectangle in the fabric like a present, as shown, and glue the fabric into place.

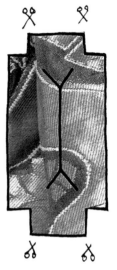

6. Cut out a rectangle from the scrap fabric, 4" (10cm) longer and wider than the cardboard rectangle cut out in step 2. Fold the fabric in half widthwise and cut a Y shape into the fabric, as shown. Then cut a 2" x 2" (5cm x 5cm) square into each corner of the fabric.

7. Center the fabric piece cut out in step 6 over the rectangular hole in the box. Fold the fabric around the edges of the rectangular opening to cover, securing with hot glue. There should be a bit of fabric hanging over the edges of the box. Glue the edges down flat on the box sides.

8. Cut a 2" x 5" (5cm x 12.5cm) rectangle from the remaining scrap fabric. **Hem** the 2 long sides of the strip. Also cut out a circle of fabric 3 times the diameter of your bottle cap. (We will use these later).

9. Cut out a 24" x 16" (61cm x 40.5cm) rectangle from the remaining fabric.

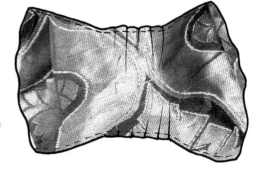

10. Make 5 **tucks** in the center of both long sides of the fabric cut out in the previous step, about ¾" (2cm) apart, and **pin** into place. Fold the long edges of the fabric over ½" (13mm) and sew all the way across both tucked edges, sewing the tucks into place.

11. Place the box in the center of the fabric, with the rectangular hole facing up and the long sides of the box parallel with the long sides of the fabric. Glue the tucked edges flush to the 2 long sides of the box, as shown.

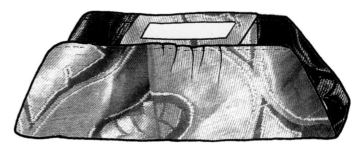

12. Glue the short edges of the fabric to the 2 short sides of the box so the entire top edge of the box is wrapped in fabric. Take the loose corners and pin them to the center top edge of the box. **Hand-stitch** the corners into place. The box should be entirely draped in fabric, and the basic shape of the bag should be in place.

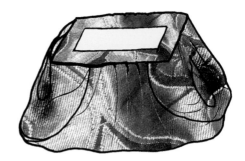

13. Place the open hinges on 1 long edge of the bag, each of them 1" (2.5cm) from the side of the box. Using a needle and thread, sew through the holes in the hinges and through the box itself to attach the hinges to the bag. Then reinforce the stitching with glue. Now place the lid on top of the box and repeat the same process to secure the lid to the box.

14. Fix the drawer pull to the center of the cardboard lid using the same technique: Sew through the holes (you may need a thimble here) and reinforce with hot glue.

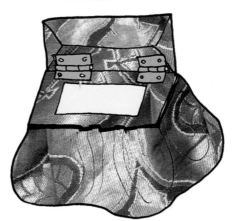

15. Place the bottle cap in the center of the fabric circle cut out in step 8. Using a needle and thread, sew ½" (13mm) from the edge of the circle, all the way around the perimeter, and then pull the thread tight to cover the bottle cap tightly and entirely, creating a covered button.

16. To keep the bag closed while it's being carried, sew the covered button onto the front center of the bag, about 1" (2.5cm) from the top edge. Glue each end of the small, hemmed fabric strip cut out in step 8 onto the inside of the lid, 1" (2.5cm) to the left and right of the center, as shown. (Double check that it's long enough to go over the button before gluing it on.) Add a couple of stitches to reinforce.

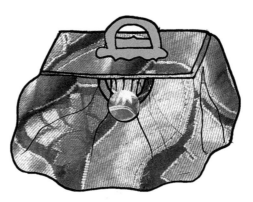

UPSCALE MEETS UPCYCLE

Sure you can bring a pancake mix box to the breakfast table, but who's crazy enough to bring one to dinner at a Park Avenue restaurant? Well with a high-class fabric wrap, that boring box can be magically transformed into a bag that will catch the eye of neighboring tables—for all the right reasons!

QUICK TIP: We used the bottom of a '70s-era disco-glam dress to make this bag. Voluminous dresses are an upcycler's dream because there is just so much fabric. We made a brand-new dress and this matching purse all from one $12 thrift-store find.

RECYCLE IT: Did you know that cardboard is reportedly the largest single source of recovered paper, making up 54 percent of all such paper in the United States?

GLITTER-MUCH CLUTCH

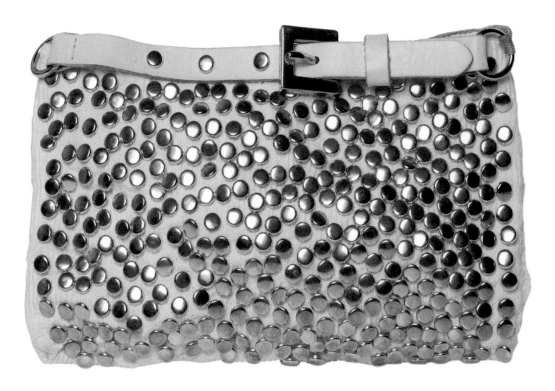

YOU'LL NEED

- 400 paper fasteners
- 1 old skinny belt
- 1 magnetic button
- 20" x 24" (51cm x 61cm) remnant of upholstery fabric
- Pins
- Thick, nylon thread
- 2 key rings, ½" (13mm) diameter

DIMENSIONS

9½" x 6" (24cm x 15cm)

1. Fold the upholstery fabric in half lengthwise and lay it down flat. Mark the fabric with pins into 4 equal-sized sections, each 10" x 6" (25.5cm x 15cm).

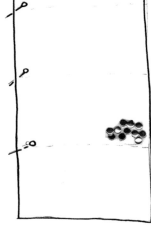

2. Now that you have divided your fabric into 4 sections, fill the third section from the top with paper fasteners by puncturing the fabric with the fastener, and then splitting apart the metal prongs to fasten it against the back of the fabric. Make sure to leave a 1" (2.5cm) margin on the left and right sides of the fabric and to reserve 20 fasteners for final embellishment. Feel free to create patterns with your fasteners, or fill up the entire section, as shown.

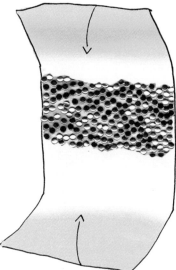

3. Fold the fabric in half widthwise with the paper fasteners on the inside, and sew the short edges of the fabric together, with a **clean finish,** to create a tube.

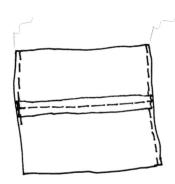

4. Fold the tube so that the newly sewn seam is in the center of the fabric, as shown. Now sew the side ends, making sure to flatten the first seam as you sew, and leave a 3" (7.5cm) opening to turn the fabric right side out.

5. Turn the fabric right side out so the paper fasteners are on the outside. **Hand-stitch** the 3" (7.5cm) gap closed, tucking in the raw edges as you go.

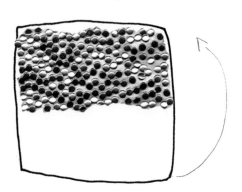
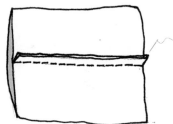

FASTENING FASHION

There is nothing quite like the joy and splendor of making beautiful things out of mundane objects—and it doesn't get much more mundane than a good ol' paper fastener. Though once ubiquitous in the office landscape, most paper fasteners now languish in desk drawers and supply closets. What's a crafty girl to do? Free the fastener! In a few short lunch hours you'll have a smashing clutch that can't wait for Friday.

QUICK TIP: Bring a paper fastener with you when scavenging for fabric. You want to be sure it's not too thick to pierce with the sharp end of the paper fastener.

RECYCLE IT: Because paper fasteners are often made of brass, they are perfect for recycling. In some communities, unneeded paper clips and fasteners fetch around 40 cents an ounce. So, check with your local recycling centers before tossing any leftovers into the trash.

6. Now fold the fabric lengthwise again and sew the sides closed with a clean finish, creating the general shape of the clutch.

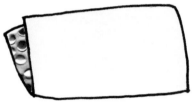

7. Sew the pieces of the magnetic button onto opposite sides of the inside center of the purse ½" (13mm) from the top edge.

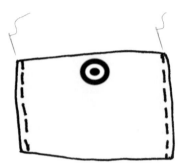

8. Cut off the ends of the skinny belt so you are left with the center piece that is 12" (30.5cm) long.

9. Create loops at each end of the center belt piece by folding 1" (2.5cm) of the ends of the belt toward the back, then hand-stitch the ends to the belt using the thick, nylon thread. (Depending on the material of your belt, you may need a thimble for this step).

10. Place the key rings onto the loops that you just created. Now insert paper fasteners into the holes of the belt but do not fasten them.

11. Place your belt along the top front edge of your clutch. Insert the paper fasteners through the fabric and fasten them to the inside of your bag. Using nylon thread, secure the belt by stitching the key rings to the bag.

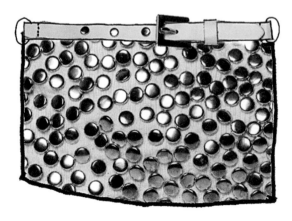

ZILLA {designer feature}

Sylvia Pichler's bags look like a high-fashion science experiment. At a glance, her bags are classic in form and proportion, but when you take a closer look—or even better, touch them—therein lies their mystique.

While studying architecture, Pichler began exploring various materials with which to make scaled models for her projects. "It is through my passion to take materials and reappropriate their use that my first bag was born," she says. Now, instead of sourcing her materials at fabric or leather wholesalers, as many designers do, she finds her materials at building and packaging tradeshows. "I often get funny looks when I ask, 'Do you happen to have different colors for this motor filter?'"

When making bags from unconventional materials, remember that you will most likely need to employ unconventional tools. Instead of needles and scissors, you may need an industrial staple gun or a riveting machine.

Stroll down the isles of your local hardware store or even the cleaning-supply section of the grocery store to search for unconventional crafting materials. Sylvia makes bags from sponges and cork. What could you make from a pair of rubber gloves, or a hose?

Name
Sylvia Pichler

Company
Zilla

URL
zilla.it

Occupation
Fashion Designer

Location
Bolzano, Italy

Bag Description
Upcycled bags made of industrial materials such as air filters, cork, vinyl mats, and sponge

Philosophy
"My bag is my castle."

Inspiration
"I am fascinated by non-conventional materials."

MAGABAG

YOU'LL NEED

- About 16 magazine pages, 8½" x 11" (21.5cm x 28cm) plus pages to cut for decoration

- School glue

- 1 chain, 34" (86cm) long

- 2 jump rings

- A drawer knob

- Mod-Podge, or a transparent acylic medium

- 1" x 1" (2.5cm x 2.5cm) cardboard

DIMENSIONS

6" x 9" x 1½" (15cm x 23cm x 3.8cm)

1. Carefully cut 12 magazine pages vertically into 3 equal-sized strips.

2. In a bowl, mix 2 parts water with 1 part school glue.

3. Dip 1 entire magazine strip into the water-glue mixture. After the strip is saturated with glue, fold 1 long edge about ¾" (2cm) in toward the center. Fold again, and continue folding until you have a thin strip about ¾" x 11" (2cm x 28cm). Hold the strip beween your thumb and index finger over the bowl. Starting at the top of the strip and sliding down vertically, gently squeeze out any excess glue. This will create a long, thin but sturdy strip.

x12

4. Repeat step 3 until you have made about 45 sturdy strips, then set strips to dry (about 30 minutes).

5. Cut 10 of the dry strips in half horizontally so you have 20 strips that are each 5½" (14cm) long.

6. Attach 1 long strip and 1 short strip together using a stapler. Repeat for the 19 remaining short strips to make a total of 20 strips that are 16½" (42cm) long.

7. Cut 20 small 1" x 2" (2.5cm x 5cm) rectangles from a magazine page. Dip 1 rectangle into the glue mixture, then wrap the rectangle around one of the staples to cover it. Repeat for all the 16½" (42cm) strips. Set to dry.

8. Lay out fifteen, 11"- (28cm-) long strips horizontally. Weave the first 16½" (42cm) strip vertically through the 11" (28cm) strips. Leave about 2" (5cm) on each side and on the left. Staple the first woven piece into place on each horizontal strip.

9. Continue to weave all the remaining 16½" (42cm) strips through the horizontal strips, alternating "over and under" and "under and over" until you have what looks like a woven place mat.

10. Staple around the 3 sides of the mat that have not yet been stapled.

11. Fold all the strip ends on the shorter sides inward in the same direction, and staple them down, creating 2 straight edges.

12. Fold the mat in half widthwise, but do not flatten the 2 sides together—doing so will create an envelope instead of a bag!

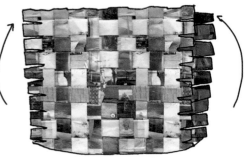

13. On both sides of the mat, fold the ends of the strips toward each other so that they overlap. Staple the overlapping strips together, starting at the bottom of the bag and working your way up to the top.

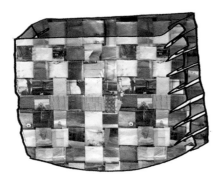

14. Weave one 11" (28m) strip into the side, leaving a loop at the top, as shown. Staple into place (use several staples to be sure the loops are secure). Repeat on the other side.

15. Cut out small, colorful images from the magazine. These will decorate the bag and cover all visible staples. Dip the images into the glue mixture, then smooth them onto the bag where the staples are visible.

16. Make 2 thin strips following the instuctions in step 3 but using undiluted glue, making sure that each fits into the jump rings. The undiluted glue will add strength. Set to dry.

17. Hook the thin strips through the larger side loops and staple in place, then cover the staples using the technique from step 7. Take 1 jump ring, open it, link it to both a loop and an end of the chain, then close the jump ring. Repeat with the remaining jump ring, and the other loop and the other end of the chain.

18. Pull the 4" (10cm) chain through the back center of the bag, 1" (2.5cm) from the top. Close the chain with a jump ring, creating a loop that will go over the knob (make sure it fits over the knob before proceeding to the next step.)

19. Glue the last few magazine pieces over the chain where it meets the bag to secure it into place.

20. Paint the entire bag inside and out with Mod-Podge or a transparent acrylic medium. Set to dry.

21. Screw the drawer knob into the front center of the bag, 1½" (3.8cm) from the top. Once the screw is poking into the inside, puncture it first through a 1" x 1" (2.5cm x 2.5cm) piece of cardboard, then put the nut on. Feel free to adjust the length of the strap by knotting the chain.

RIP GLOSS

The Magabag is one of those special accessories that can spice up any outfit. Its color weave makes the bag playful while the long chain strap allows for adjustability and adds a touch of glitz.

QUICK TIP: Go monochromatic using pages from a novel. The black type will give your bag a sophisticated, graphic look. Just remember that smaller strips will create a smaller bag, so plan your design accordingly.

NOT SO FUN FACT: Today in America, only 20 percent of magazines from the home are recycled, though two-thirds of the population have access to magazine recycling.

DOLCE DOILY PURSE

YOU'LL NEED

- 6 curtain rings
- 3 colors of cloth ribbon, about 6.7yd (6.1m)
- 2 small strips of suede or other strong, glue-able fabric
- 2 crocheted doilies, 2 small and 2 large (We used diameters of about 6" (15cm) and 10" (25.5cm).)
- Pins

DIMENSIONS

19" x 8" (48.5cm x 20.5cm)

1. Cut 1 yard (91cm) of ribbon. Tie a knot around 1 curtain ring with the ribbon. Begin to wrap the ribbon onto the ring, through the ring's hole, making sure the ribbon lies flat. Continue this process until the ring is completely covered by the ribbon, adding a dollop of hot glue onto the ribbon every so often to keep it in place.

2. Repeat step 1 until you have covered all 6 rings.

3. Tie the end of a ribbon onto a matching ring. Once secure, take another ring and tie the ribbon to it as well, so that the 2 rings are touching at the knots. Thread the ribbon up through the first ring, then down through the second ring. Wrap the ribbon around the rings in this fashion 5 times or until the ribbon holds the rings together tightly. Then, wrap the ribbon around the center point between the 2 rings multiple times, tying knots occasionally, until the rings feel securely knotted together.

4. Repeat step 3 until all of the rings are attached to one another in a row.

5. Fold 1 of the larger doilies in half. (If any of your doilies are slightly larger, use the largest doily for this step.) **Whipstitch** around the perimeter of the doily about 6" (15cm) up each side, starting from the corners, to make a pouch with an opening at the top.

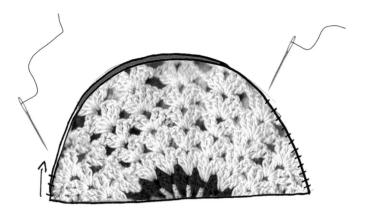

6. Fold 1 of the smaller doilies over the corner of the pouch, placing it at about a 70-degree angle. **Pin** into place. **Hand-stitch** it onto the corner. Repeat on the other side with the other small doily.

7. Fold the remaining doily evenly over the top of the bag. Pin the doily to the bag only on the back.

8. Cover 1 end of a 2'- (61cm-) long ribbon with a bit of masking tape, like a shoelace, to facilitate threading. Tie the ribbon to one of the crochet loops in the top of the bag where the top doily meets the side doily. Weave the ribbon through the crochet loops in the lace of the top doily and center doily, to secure the top doily onto the body of the bag. Remove the masking tape and pins.

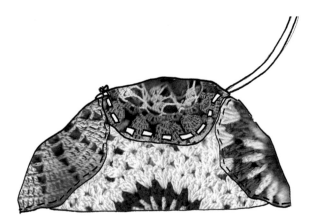

9. Thread each small suede strip through a crochet loop at each side of the bag, where the top doily meets the side doilies.

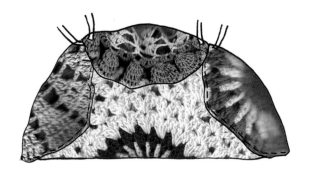

10. Loop the suede around the first covered ring and glue the ends together to create a loop. Repeat on the other side . . . and voilà!

ALL HOOKED UP

Your grandmother may tell you that doilies were once commonplace in every home, used as mats underneath plates and bowls. These days, doilies are relics of the past. Lucky for us, that makes them pretty easy to find and perfect for repurposing. Check out local estate sales and thrift stores to find doilies of all sizes— or you could just swipe a few from your grandma.

QUICK TIP: Old cotton doilies are often yellowed with age, but don't despair. Depending on the type of stain, fabric dye may be able to make any unsightly spots disappear.

RECYCLE IT: Have a few leftover doilies? Create a fabulous little makeup bag. Sew together the edges of 2 doilies of similar circumference, leaving a 4" (10cm) opening. Then turn it inside out to sew a zipper into the opening. Turn your bag right-side out and fill it with your favorite cosmetics.

G-LOVE CLUTCH

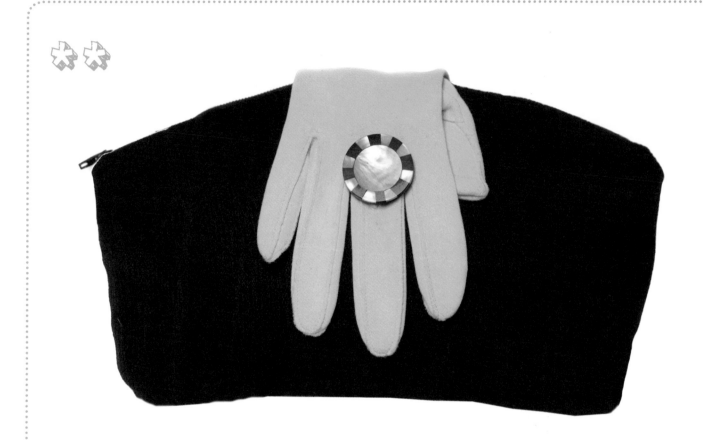

YOU'LL NEED

- 1 glove
- 1 vintage button
- 10" (25.5cm) zipper
- 2 scraps of fabric, at least 10" x 6" (25.5cm x 15cm) each
- Pins

DIMENSIONS

9" x 5" (23cm x 12.5cm)

1. Measure the center on one of the fabric scraps and mark it with chalk. Draw a line down from the center marking to the bottom of the fabric on the inside. Measure 1" (2.5cm) from the center line on each side along the bottom and cut tiny slits in the fabric there.

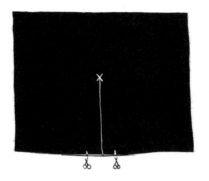

2. Fold the fabric in half widthwise (right side facing inward) and sew a straight line from the tiny slits to the center marking, creating a **dart**. Repeat steps 1–2 for the remaining scrap.

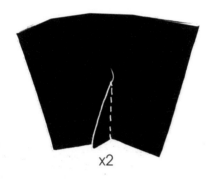

x2

3. Open each piece of fabric. With the dart facing downward, hem the top edges of each piece.

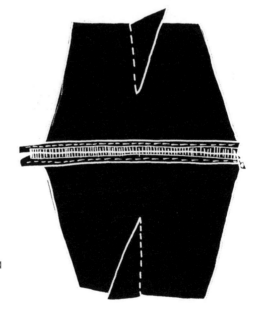

4. Using a zipper foot on the sewing machine, sew the zipper onto the 2 long edges of the fabric pieces with a **clean finish**.

HANDY 'N' DANDY

The glove, that dainty accessory that women once wore for high tea, has slipped into a sad state of total disuse. Think about it: When was the last time you saw a woman wear gloves out and about? Well, fear not, fashionistas; this clutch will breathe new life into that once iconic accessory while turning a banal black clutch into an unforgettable showpiece.

QUICK TIP: Use a thin glove for your clutch in a color that contrasts with the purse so your bag really pops.

RECYCLE IT: If you have more gloves than could ever be made into clutches, don't despair. Gloves make ironic/iconic embellishments for clothing, accessories, and even furniture. Sew a pair onto the ends of a long thin scarf, or onto the seat of a chair!

5. Place the 2 rectangles face to face (darts facing downward) and sew the 3 remaining edges together. Cut off the darts and turn right side out.

6. **Make an appropriately sized buttonhole** in the glove at the knuckle of the middle finger. (The buttonhole size depends upon the size of your button and should go through both layers of the glove.)

7. Drape the glove over the top of the bag so that the thumb and 5 fingers are draped over the front and the wrist is in the back. **Pin** into place. **Topstitch** the glove onto the back to secure it.

8. **Sew the button** onto the bag so that it fits through the button-hole.

QUICK FIXES

There are so many bags in the world that are in great shape but might not be the right color or don't have that special something that makes a bag spectacular. These quick fixes will show you how to take existing bags and, with a little glue or a little paint, make 'em what they ain't!

➕ Add a new handle made of buttons! Use a pair of pliers to help weave a thin, pliable wire through the holes in vintage buttons, leaving wire on 1 end (the length should be the length of your bag plus 2 inches). Now cut a strip of fabric almost the full length of your bag and an inch wide. Sew the outer edges of the strip onto the inside crease of the bag between the flap and the inside of the bag (use a glue gun for leather). Thread the wire through the "tunnel" created by the strip and attach the wire ends together with a tight twist.

➕ Get busy with the hot glue gun! Cover unsightly or stained bags with fake flowers, buttons, foreign coins, or even a bamboo sushi mat! Give the bag a whole new look in a matter of minutes.

GLOSSARY OF TECHNIQUES

Clean Finish

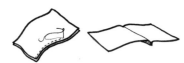

Put the right sides of the fabric together and sew a straight seam ³⁄₈" (1cm) from the edge. Then turn the right sides out so the raw edges are inside and unseen.

Create a Covered Hem

Sew a fabric strip onto the raw edge with the right sides together. Then fold the outer edge of the strip up and over the stitched edge; iron flat. Topstitch on the edge to secure the strip in place.

Create a Curved Seam

For curved seams, cut small notches along the edge at regular intervals, ½" (13mm) apart along the edge of the curve. Fold the curved edge of the fabric over ½" (13mm). Press the curve to make sure it remains nice and flat. Now topstitch around the curve, fixing the curved edge into place.

Create a Dart

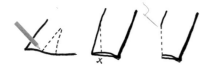

Mark out a triangle with legs of even length. Fold fabric in half, matching the legs together, and sew along one leg to the apex of the triangle. Unfold the fabric and press the dart to one side.

Create a Rolled Hem

Fold the edge 2 times (keeping the raw edge on the inside), then sew with a topstitch.

Gather

Machine sew two parallel rows of stitches along the edge of the fabric. Pull the lower threads (the bobbin threads) to make tiny folds. Stitch over the folds to secure them in place.

Gather with Elastic

Cut a piece of elastic about half the length of the fabric to be gathered. Pin the end of the elastic to the fabric and stretch the elastic with your hand while sewing over the fabric and elastic with a zigzag stitch.

Hand-Stitch

By hand, sew evenly spaced stitches with a doubled thread. Use this stitch for thick layers or delicate sewing.

Hem

Fold the edge over and stitch the folded edge flat.

Make a Buttonhole

Draw a line slightly longer than the diameter of the button to be used. Zigzag-stitch around the drawn line (not over the line). Cut an opening on the line between the stitches with sharp scissors.

Pin before Sewing

Pin fabric layers together before sewing to help keep the fabric in place.

Pleat

Make evenly spaced folds along the fabric edge (ironing folded edges helps). Pin the folds into place, then sew over folds to secure pleats.

Quilt

Evenly place soft filling between layers of fabric. Sew short stitches over the filled fabric in a square or diamond pattern.

Sew on a Button

Double a thread through a needle and knot the ends. Push the needle through the back of the fabric and through one of the holes in the buttons. Bring the needle back down through the other hole and through the fabric. Bring the needle up through the fabric and under the button. Wrap the thread three times around the threads holding the button to the fabric. Fasten with a knot underneath the fabric.

Topstitch

Place one fabric on top of the other and stitch on top through both layers.

Tuck

Make a fold along the fabric edge and stitch in place. Do not iron as for pleats.

Whipstitch

Sew stitches vertically or diagonally along the intended stitch line. This stitch is useful for finishing edges and for sewing together pieces of fabric.

Zigzag Stitch

Sew with the zigzag setting on your sewing machine. This stitch is useful for stretch fabrics and elastic.

MATERIALS INDEX

RECYCLER'S RESOURCES

Here's a selection of some of our coveted sources of inspiration and materials.

Recycled Bags:

globalexchangestore.org

globalgoodspartners.org

myrecycledbags.com

uncommongoods.com

ganesha.co.uk

greatgreengoods.com

inhabitat.com

naturalcollection.com

seabags.com

redflagdesign.ca

greenwithenvygifts.com

eco-handbags.ca

reusablebags.com

DIY Resources:

bitsandbobbins.com

burdastyle.com

craftster.org

craftzine.com

cutoutandkeep.net

ecofabulous.com

etsy.com

indiebizchicks.com

janome.com

outsapop.com

smashingdarling.com

supernaturale.com

threadbanger.com

venuszine.com

Secondhand Stores:

Goodwill Industries

International: goodwill.org

Salvation Army:

salvationarmyusa.org

Clothing Swaps:

clothingswap.org

garmentremake.com

swaporamarama.org

ACKNOWLEDGMENTS

This book was a real labor of love and would not have been possible without the help of so many talented individuals. To **Philip**: your photography captured the happy spirit of Compai, and your extreme patience and easygoing attitude made a few long days speed by. *Merci beaucoup!* To **Jenny**, **Candice, and Lauren**, thanks for lending trained eyes, so much time, tools, for help averting disaster, and for just being so RAD. To **Caits**—thanks for the help with styling, modeling, babysitting, and for ALWAYS being there when we ALWAYS need you. **Sarit**, our *principessa*, a curtsy to the floor for your generous advice, the precious time, the stunning cover, and all the good laughs. Ten dozen black orchids to Alicia for her utter brilliance, sunny disposition, and technical support. **Jason**, thanks for help with the illos and for being my favorite coworking buddy. **Mom and Dad**, thanks for all of the support and the babysitting and being the bestest bubby and popop ever. And you too, **Ga**

Ga and **Papa Cookie**. **Rosy**, **Thom**—thanks for believing in the project. **Rebecca**, **Chi Ling, Erica, La Tricia**—thanks to you and the whole team at Potter for all of the hours, the advice, the expertise, and the patience. Thank you **Melissa** and **Adam** for seeing us through this and for your patience. Thanks to all of our über-talented **featured designers** for trusting us with your bags! Thanks to the **Janome** team for providing us with the BEST sewing machines. To all the other homies and family (especially **Noa**, **Shi**, **Em**, **Eden**, **Yoshi**, **Duane**, **Ellen, and Anka**), thanks for the constant support and inspiration, then and now. A shout out to Spoonbill & Sugartown, Booksellers; The Bedford Cheese Shop, and Aurora Restaurant and Bar for providing brilliant backdrops for our photo shoot. To the Brooklyn crew, the LA crew, and Crew Italia . . . WE LOVE YOU!

ABOUT THE AUTHORS

California natives (and sisters) Justina and Faith Blakeney are the designers behind **Compai**, a crafty design studio and eco-clothing label.

With a focus on sustainable design and DIY, Compai has authored three popular craft books, they host workshops, and they collaborate with companies such as zazzle.com and etsy.com. Compai has been seen in the pages of *Vogue, Glamour, Venus Zine,* the *San Francisco Chronicle,* and on NBC's *The Today Show.*

Check out what all the fuss is about at **compai.com**.

BONUS MATERIALS

VARIATIONS: Try mixing and matching bag techniques to fashion your own designs!

1. Use the plastic bag fusion technique to make a tote using the pattern and handle from the Towel-It Tote.

2. Make the handle from the Dolce Doily Bag and add it to the Glitter-Much Clutch!

3. Use paper fasteners to transform everyday bags into evening bags! Try covering the handles of the Tux Redux Bag in paper fasteners to give it rock-star sparkle.

Handmade Handbag by _____
URL _____
_____

Use this template to make your own business cards!

Hungry for more? Check out our blog at compai.blogspot.com for tons of DIY projects and ideas to funk your junk . . . Compai style!